The Life Plan

Simple Strategies
for Building Confidence
in a Changing World

SHANNAH KENNEDY

BEYOND WORDS
Portland, Oregon

BEYOND WORDS

1750 S.W. Skyline Blvd., Suite 20
Portland, OR 97221-2543
503-531-8700 / 503-531-8773 fax
www.beyondword.com

First Beyond Words paperback edition May 2022
Previously published in 2015 in Australia under ISBN: 978-0-670-07830-1

BEYOND WORDS PUBLISHING and colophon are registered
trademarks of Beyond Words Publishing. Beyond Words is an imprint of
Simon & Schuster, Inc.

For more information about special discounts for bulk purchases,
please contact Beyond Words Special Sales at 503-531-8700 or
specialsales@beyondword.com.

Managing editor: Lindsay S. Easterbrooks-Brown
Copyeditor: Kristin Thiel
Proofreader: Olivia Rollins
Design: Sara E. Blum
Composition: William H. Brunson Typography Services
Manufactured in the United States of America

10 9 8 7 6 5 4 3 2 1

Library of Congress Cataloging-in-Publication Data:

Names: Kennedy, Shannah, author.
Title: The life plan : simple strategies for building confidence in a
   changing world / Shannah Kennedy.
Description: First Beyond Words paperback edition. | Portland, Oregon :
   Beyond Words, [2022]
Identifiers: LCCN 2021058129 (print) | LCCN 2021058130 (ebook) | ISBN
   9781582708669 (paperback) | ISBN 9781582708676 (ebook)
Subjects: LCSH: Self-actualization (Psychology) | Change (Psychology) |
   Goal (Psychology) | Self-confidence.
Classification: LCC BF637.S4 K454 2022 (print) | LCC BF637.S4 (ebook) |
   DDC 158.1—dc23/eng/20211217
LC record available at https://lccn.loc.gov/2021058129
LC ebook record available at https://lccn.loc.gov/2021058130

The corporate mission of Beyond Words Publishing, Inc.: *Inspire to Integrity*

This book is dedicated to my husband,
Michael, my soul mate.

To my children, Jack and Mia, the best
gifts I have ever received.

This book is also dedicated to you,
the reader, to my wonderful clients and
followers—may this book be your
handbook for life.

Your
thoughts create
your world.

CONTENTS

Part 3: Take Control

Part 4: Get Going

Part 5: Thrive

Part 6: Refuel

CONTENTS

Part 7: Shine

INTRODUCTION

This book shows you my simple tools to make life bigger, better, more meaningful and whole, and healthier, both personally and professionally. My approach is for optimal, calm, confident living in all areas of my life; the *business of me* is my first and foremost job—everything else comes after that.

Throughout my twenty years of coaching, I have found that most of my clients share one thing in common—they don't need motivation. They're very successful people, and they know what they need to do to reach their goals. What they actually require is for things to be simplified, so they can get back to the foundations of who they are, dig themselves out of the clutter to find fresh confidence, clarity, and purpose in their daily routines, and live a full life without self-destructing in the process. In this book, I share the tools I've developed with my clients over the years to help them do that.

My life has been a truly big journey. I think I wanted that from the day I was born. When I saw the movie *Wall Street* in 1987, I was seventeen years old and trying to decide what to do with my life. All of that power, wealth, and success was hugely appealing to my adolescent self, so I committed to getting a job at a high-profile stockbroking firm—and pulled it off. But there was increasing pressure to gain a degree, and I hated studying, so after a few years, I chose more life experience and began looking for my next chapter.

Aged twenty-one, I set off to explore the world. I backpacked around Europe, the Middle East, and parts of Africa, working my way through kitchens and bars. I slept under the stars high in the Atlas Mountains of Morocco, dozed on a small wooden boat on the river Nile, swam in the Dead Sea, and waitressed in the ski resort of Mürren, Switzerland, home of the James Bond 007 revolving restaurant. I hitchhiked through Spain, sleeping on many rooftops and staying everywhere from basic rooms to the odd grand castle. It was the most wonderful adventure.

After two years I came home and went back to the stockbroking firm, but I didn't feel challenged. Trying to be true to myself, I decided to swap numbers and stress for something completely different and took up an assistant role in a golf management company. Soon I was negotiating contracts, managing professional golfers, traveling on tours, organizing corporate golf days, and learning everything there was to know about running a business from the ground up. It was a time of major growth.

Then, as often happens when you least expect it, life threw me a curveball, and I was asked to join a high-profile sports eyewear company as their sponsorship and PR manager. Overnight I went from managing a dozen golfers to working with more than one hundred world-class athletes in Australia and internationally. By most people's definition of success, I was living the dream. It was exhilarating, satisfying, and demanding all at once. It was also incredibly intense.

As a high achiever, I was used to overloading my life, so when the stress and exhaustion mounted, I brushed these warning signs aside as the price to be paid for the kind of success I craved. I believed I was strong and nothing was going to hold me back from having everything I wanted. I was both unwilling and unable to slow down, and eventually my body delivered a devastating reminder of its need to be cared for, abruptly giving way to chronic fatigue syndrome (CFS).

It was debilitating. Virtually bedridden for twelve months, I lost everything that mattered to me—my sense of self, my network, my ability to do the simplest things. My body just wouldn't respond. Sinking toward depression, I felt overwhelmed with shame and failure, replaying why things had gone so wrong over and over in my mind.

It took me a long, slow three years to fully recover, but with help from a life coach, I eventually regained my energy, clarity, and motivation to move on. It took several more years before I realized what a blessing my illness really was—a gift that allowed me to see life's grand picture.

I have also (unforgettably) witnessed many elite athletes self-destruct once their sporting careers were over. This, as well as my own experience with burnout, inspired me to get over my distaste for study and embrace extensive training to become an advanced certified coach. Who would have known I could be a committed student? I could see an opportunity to coach sportspeople to become whole people rather than has-beens, with the purpose and vision to create the life they want, both during and after their (relatively) short athletic careers.

During this productive time, I loved taking myself away to health retreats to recuperate and recharge. I recognized that I also needed to find a way to integrate these stress-busting, restorative strategies into my everyday life. It's no good if you can only find that clarity when you're away from your ordinary life. So, I have tried and tested strategies to get that balance—to find depth and calm in my work, joy and contentment in my family, and vitality and vibrancy in my life. To build a rock-solid foundation based on my purpose and a valuable, personal definition of success to guide my choices and behaviors as I go through life. To do whatever I can and live without regrets.

Over a decade on, my passion for managing time so it works for us, rather than against us, means my services are in constant demand. We all want a good life, but this has become increasingly challenging for many of us as we're mentally ambushed at work and over-connected digitally and yet under-connected in our most important relationships.

Working within large corporations coaching senior executives, sales teams, individual business owners, and contractors, I always focus on the foundations. By going back to the basics, we can regain control and therefore make clear, informed decisions and also build supportive habits to create lives we love living.

Over the years, the structures that are outlined in this book have guided strategies for employee engagement, inspired valuable team-building activities, and provided powerful tools to connect leaders with their teams. They have proven to be effective not only for managers, leaders, entrepreneurs, and business owners but anyone who wants to set and achieve clear goals, create success on their own terms, foster meaningful relationships, and live each day to the fullest, with a sense of depth, strength, and sustainability. They have empowered every client I have coached, whether they are a stay-at-home mom, small-business operator, multimillionaire, or elite athlete.

With all this going on, my life was soon humming along: happy marriage, two healthy children at school, the house renovated, and my business booming. My first book, *Simplify Structure Succeed*, was in its third print run, having proven itself to be a tool my clients loved. The seeds I'd planted along my journey were all coming into bloom. So, I decided it was the perfect time to shut up shop—at least for a few months.

It was time to press the pause button on life, to get the courage to walk away from all that was comfortable, to grow, to connect with myself and my family unit at a whole different level, all while facing the possibility that my business might be gone by the time we came home. Our mini-sabbatical of five months away was an investment in our life strategy, a serious mental and physical deposit into our lives to avoid burnout and mental fatigue. I share this story in the book, and I have committed to taking mini-breaks on an ongoing basis, rather than waiting to retire to live my life's adventures.

This book is for your life strategy, to help you get back to your foundations, to understand what life looks like at your best, and to prepare your future intentions so the road ahead is clear, inspiring, and full of success.

This book is about integrating the things that most people only discover when they hit rock bottom into your everyday life, now. It is about taking things one day at a time so you can start forming habits that become a way of life and giving each moment the potential to take you closer to the way you want to live. It is your personal life coach. It is a place to plan, visualize, reflect, and prioritize. It is a place to start, simplify, and succeed. A place for the fundamental work to be done. It is a practical guide to effective life planning.

Yours in intentional, optimal living,

Shannah

PS. Remember, it is not just about what you get by accomplishing your goals and achieving success but also about who you become through the process.

Get out of the
passenger seat
and into the
driver's seat.
Driving is a blast!

Part 1

Reflect

Knowing yourself is the beginning of all wisdom.

Aristotle, Greek philosopher

Look Inward

Who are you? This is one of the first questions I ask every new client, and the incredible thing is, most cannot answer it. Many of us rely on our work to define our sense of ourselves, but I ask clients to think about who they are outside of that.

You might be a CEO, an entrepreneur, an executive, an office worker, or a creative artist, but while this is what you do, at the end of the day, it's not who you are. Parent, employee, boss, landlord, partner, husband, wife, investor, client, friend, sister, uncle, business owner, soccer coach, coffee aficionado . . . These are all examples of the many different hats we wear in our everyday lives. But these are roles we play, rather than who we are at our very core.

Finding out exactly who you are away from all these tasks and roles is liberating and offers insight into whether you're on track or perhaps way off it. The question is actually less "Who am I?" and more "Who am I without my job, partner, home, car, hobbies, kids, and family?" This is how we start our confidence journey.

At your current stage of life, you have had a tapestry of valuable life experiences. Some will have been great, some good, others okay, and no doubt some will have been bad, but each one has shaped who you are today. Together they provide you with all the information you need to tell you who you are and who you want to be.

I've left plenty of blank pages for you to jot notes in while you read, answer questions presented throughout the book, write affirmations for yourself, and start making plans for your life, but I also recommend you keep a journal within reach. You'll probably have a lot to think about. This book is a prompt to get you thinking and planning what your life can and will look like.

The Story of
Your Life So Far

Take a quick look at how you got to this point in your life, without getting caught up in the emotion of past experiences. Simply write down the experiences that have shaped you the most as a person.

Your life timeline:

0 ———————————————————————————

———————————————————————————

10 ———————————————————————————

———————————————————————————

15

20

25

30

35

40

45

50

55

60

65

70

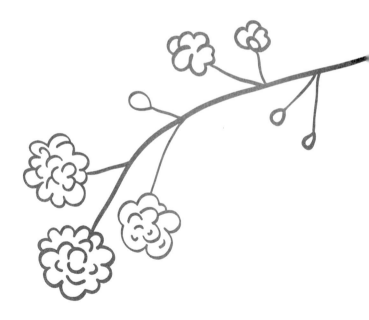

Discover Who
You Are

Every action we take is preceded by a question, whether we know it or not. It could be as simple as: "Do I want to do this?" Yet often we're completely unaware of the questions we ask ourselves or how they shape our lives.

Learning to tune in to this question is one of the most powerful ways to start finding the insight, inspiration, and authenticity to live the life you really want. It cuts through the fog and overload in your mind to give clarity and simplify the picture of who you are and what you are trying to achieve. It also builds your self-esteem and confidence as you discover that many of the answers you are seeking lie within.

These questions will help you get started on the process of clearly defining who you are. Take time to consider each question fully and honestly, as they provide the framework that you will later use to establish your values.

Who/what is most important to you?

_____

_____

Who/what are you inspired by and why?

_____

_____

What makes you smile or brings you sheer delight?

_____

_____

When have you felt you were at your best, most passionate, and most alive?

_____

_____

What are your natural gifts and abilities?

_____

_____

What do you like about yourself?

_____

_____

What mistakes have you learned from?

_____

_____

What hardships have you overcome?

_____

_____

What are you afraid of?

_____

_____

How do you want to be remembered by your friends and family?

_____

_____

What do you really want for your future?

_____

_____

Who do you need permission from to start taking responsibility?

_____

_____

What are you choosing to do?

_____

_____

What areas of your life do you most want to move forward in?

_____

_____

Make a pact with yourself to be you and no one else.
Be proud of and own who you are.

Who Are You When You're at Your Best?

Are you clear about what's true, good, and possible when it comes to who you are? Unfortunately, many of us tend to dwell on our failures. Stories of our worst moments tend to linger far too long, while stories of our best moments fade all too fast. Most of us are so busy churning along on the treadmill of everyday life that we tend to gloss over our achievements.

Take a moment to think back on the last few times you felt you were really engaged, energized, and enjoying your life.

What was happening?

_____

_____

What were you doing at the time?

_____

_____

Who were you with?

_____

_____

How did it feel to be this person?

_____

_____

Why are you proud of this moment?

_____

_____

These might be big or small moments. They might be at work, at home, or at play. They might be long or short moments. Every moment at your best is worth remembering, as it helps you find ways to spend more time being who you're capable of being.

When you understand and own your best moments, you improve your sense of confidence and your ability to create more moments like these. Savoring your successes allows you to build your confidence, fuel your optimism, and motivate yourself to keep moving on.

Often people attempt to live their lives backwards; they try to have more things, or more money, in order to do more of what they want so they will be happier. The way it actually works is the reverse. You must first BE who you really are, then DO what you need to do, in order to HAVE what you want.

Margaret Young, American singer and comedian

Clarify Your Purpose

Of all the questions I ask myself, by far the most powerful is the one that I start with each morning: What is my purpose today?

My purpose in life is to live it fully and to make the most of what I have been given. But when I break it down daily by asking, "What is my purpose today?" I make real leaps forward in my level of happiness and sense of achievement.

To have purpose is to feel connected to something bigger than ourselves—be it a religion, community, sporting club, or cause. It's a reason to get out of bed each morning. It gives us something to aim for and helps to clarify our intentions. It also inspires us and makes our heart and soul warm with excitement.

For some of us, purpose is grounded in popularity, power, and money. For others, the focus is growth and contribution. What matters most is that we pursue our purpose for the right reasons—because it's something we deeply believe in, rather than something someone else is steering us toward. Knowing your purpose helps you live life with integrity.

Questions to Discover Your Purpose

- What do you love to do?

- What comes easily to you?

- What are your strengths that you like expressing in the world?

- How do you want to feel each day?

- How do you want to be remembered, and what can you do to be that person?

- What messages do you want to give your children?

- What difference will others say you made in this world?

- What do you want to achieve in your life?

- How do you want to feel as you move through each day?

- When you are your best possible self, who might you be?

- How can you serve others?

When we know our purpose, we move from "what I do" to "why I am doing it." And remember, your life counts, your voice matters, your story is important, your kindness is contagious, and your spark ignites others.

Touching base each day with the essential powerful questions to keep you connected with your mindset, your heart space, your purpose, and your inspired self is a habit worth cultivating.

Define
Your Values

Defining your values is the next major step to unlocking your success. Values are those things that really matter to you—the ideas and beliefs you deem to be the most important in your life.

A range of factors, including your background, your upbringing, your spiritual beliefs, your life philosophy, and events that you've experienced or witnessed, all shape the values you hold. Values have a major influence on your behavior and serve as broad guidelines to make authentic choices that leave you feeling more content, happy, and satisfied as life unfolds. When your actions aren't in alignment with your values, you find yourself without a sense of achievement or feeling out of control.

The best day of your life is the day on which you decide to own your set of values and live by them. Do you know what your values are? Are you living your life accordingly?

Getting clear on your own set of values enables you to make calm, confident decisions. Values allow you to be true to yourself and love with authenticity. Values are what matter to you most and influence your personal attitude, outlook, and behavior. Values are the underlying motivators of life. Values are your foundation, your home base, the boss, and your code of conduct for making decisions.

Your values and purpose provide you with meaning, clarity, and direction each day. They provide a framework to get you in touch—with what you do, how you do it, and why you do it.

My Top Three Values

My top three values are health (physical and mental), the happiness of my family, and having a sense of achievement daily. Understanding my values brings absolute clarity to every decision I make.

The characteristics I want to project are calm, confidence, and fun. I aim to keep my body strong, to travel with purpose, to keep my marriage wholehearted, connected, and inspirational, and to support my business by constantly evolving and growing my skill set and adapting to the changing world.

18

In the past, my sense of achievement was gained from doing more—being more efficient and more productive and succeeding in sport and business. However, it has evolved to include the more nourishing elements of space; valuing the downtime and conscious refueling activities—such as breath work, journaling, and meditation—just as much as the busy times helps me have a long and sustainable career.

Make a deliberate and conscious effort to identify,
and live according to, your values.

Defining Your Values

Select: Identify your top ten values, choosing from the box of ideas I suggest here. Don't spend too much time agonizing over your decisions: go with your gut instinct.

Prioritize: Prioritize each value from one to ten. Focus on your top five and briefly define what each one means to you.

Contemplate: Read each value slowly, letting the meaning of each word sink in so that you fully understand what each one means to you.

Define: Select your top three values and write them down. Commit them to memory, as they will now act as your decision-making blueprint. You also need to define the single value that is most important to you.

Commit: Work out what you need to add or remove from your life and what you need to change to reflect these values.

Family Happiness Quality time, bonding	**Self-Respect** Sense of personal identity, pride	**Generosity** Helping others, improving society
Competitiveness Winning, taking risks	**Recognition** Acknowledgment, status	**Wisdom** Discovering and understanding knowledge
Friendship Close relationships with others	**Advancement** Promotions	**Spirituality** Strong religious and/or spiritual beliefs
Affection Love, caring	**Health** Mental, physical	**Loyalty** Devotion, trustworthiness
Cooperation Working well with others, teamwork	**Responsibility** Being accountable for results	**Culture** Traditions, customs, beliefs

Adventure New challenges	**Fame** Public recognition	**Inner Harmony** Being at peace
Achievement A sense of accomplishment	**Involvement** Belonging, being involved with others	**Order** Stability, conformity, tranquillity
Wealth Getting rich, making money	**Economic Security** Strong and consistent income streams	**Creativity** Being imaginative, innovative
Energy Vitality, vim, vigor	**Pleasure** Fun, laughter, a leisurely lifestyle	**Integrity** Honesty, sincerity, standing up for oneself
Freedom Independence, autonomy	**Power** Control, authority, or influence over others	**Personal Development** Use of personal potential

I program my phone to greet me with my values each morning.
It is an instant reminder that all my decisions need to be in alignment
with my values. They then become confident decisions,
and I become a confident decision-maker.

Identify
Lessons Learned

What have been your greatest life lessons so far? The purpose of asking this question is not to become lost in introspection. Rather, it is to prevent you from making the same mistakes so that you can grow, evolve, and continue to learn.

Your greatest lessons help to shape you into the person you are, and although they can be painful, many lessons ultimately make life more enjoyable and rewarding.

For instance, after suffering from chronic fatigue syndrome that was brought on by trying to achieve too much, I learned that whenever I say yes to anything—a job, an opportunity, a favor, or an invitation—there is a cost involved. So, I need to be aware of that cost, whether it is to my health, family time, or finances, before making any decisions.

Are your problems recurring ones from the past? They become habits and a pattern when we don't stop to acknowledge them, address them, and learn from them. Creating a strategy so they don't happen again is critical. Why does the same thing keep happening to you? Do you really care enough to do something about it once and for all? How can you now make a difference?

Emotionally intelligent leaders strive to learn from mistakes because they know how valuable they are for growth—personal and professional—and your ability to move forward.

Your greatest lessons help to shape you into the person you are.

Some Popular Lessons

- When in doubt, just take the next small step.

- Don't take yourself so seriously.

- Pay off your credit cards each month.

- You don't have to win every argument. Agree to disagree.

- Cry with someone. It's more healing than crying alone.

- Make peace with your past, so you don't bring it into your future.

- Don't compare your life with the lives of others. You have no idea what their journey is about.

- A writer writes. If you want to be a writer, write.

- It is never too late to have a happy childhood. But the second childhood is up to you.

- Pop that bottle of champagne; wear your fanciest clothes. Don't save them for a special occasion.

- Overprepare and then go with the flow.

- Find joy now. Allow yourself to expand your creative side.

- Frame every so-called disaster with these words: Will this matter in five years?

- However good or bad a situation is, it will change.

- Get outside every day. Miracles are waiting everywhere.

- Take a deep breath. It calms the mind.

- Ask and be open to receiving.

Acknowledge Your Golden Moments

What are the memories you treasure? These are tiny snapshots for you to take daily; they're to be cherished and archived in your mind forever. There is gold around you all the time if you choose to look for it, engage, and be present. This is what gives depth to our lives.

- Noticing the first blossom on a tree

- Walking out of an interview or meeting and knowing you nailed it

- Gazing at the stars

- Feeling the sand between your toes at the beach
- Noticing the shape of water as it drips down a window
- Catching a glimpse of your lover daydreaming
- Seeing the sacred geometry in a perfectly formed flower
- Hearing your child in deep laughter
- Appreciating the moment of someone playing beautiful music
- Being promoted or offered a new job
- Noticing the smell of really good coffee
- Passing a test or exam with flying colors
- Connecting with your pet
- Closing your eyes and listening to the birds sing
- Tuning in to your sense of sound when you first wake up
- Noticing the seasons changing
- The feeling of fresh sheets on the bed
- The joy and energy you feel when dancing to your favorite song

This simple act of mindfulness, of tuning in and being truly present to the small wonders unfolding all around you, while calmly acknowledging and accepting your thoughts, feelings, and bodily sensations, is an oasis you can tap into anywhere, at any time.

Look for, and savor, the golden moments happening all around you, each and every day, and use them to guide your vision of success.

To be mindful means to dwell deeply in the present moment.

Write Your Definition of Success

Before you start striving for success, it's important to identify exactly what it means to you. And just as importantly, how you will measure the way success is unfolding in your life.

There's no right or wrong way to define success—it is simply what matters most to you. It's crucial to identify your own criteria because achieving success (and feeling successful) is where you want to invest your energy and effort on a daily basis.

How does success feel to you?

_____

_____

How do you define success, in one sentence?

_____

_____

How will you measure it daily?

_____

_____

What we're after is a new, sustainable formula for success that allows you to embrace everything you are today. We make a huge number of choices on a day-to-day basis that determine how successful we are, and it is up to you to recognize this. Tapping into your feeling of success every day will keep you motivated and inspired. Here are examples of what success may mean to you:

- Success means freedom of choice in my daily life.

- Success is the ability to earn a living from work that I'm passionate about.

- Success means living a purposeful life.

- Success is when I approve of myself and what I'm doing each day.

EXAMPLE

Max's Success

For my client Max, success is defined in three critical ways. As a research scientist, he believes that success means being ahead of his peers and being widely published. It means mastering new technology at work and making sure he has time to get to the gym. He also measures his success every day in terms of daily tasks like always making his bed, checking in with his dad, and making sure he reads something enjoyable for at least twenty minutes a day. I love how he sees the big picture as well as the little details to define success.

EXAMPLE

Amanda's Success

For Amanda, success at the moment is tied up in her attempts to conceive a child. Success to her means having a baby; however, we have worked together to broaden her definition of success, especially on a daily basis, to ensure that her own self-care and self-love, family, friends, work, and lifestyle are not forgotten. Success for Amanda became about taking fantastic care of herself, eating well (not too much Netflix!), keeping fit, catching up with friends, beach walks with her mom and sister, great sleep hygiene, and embracing complementary medicine to reduce the side effects of the IVF treatment. Overall, we were able to redefine success beyond the conception of a child, opening up to possibilities of a great life even if IVF is not successful.

Remember and own your proudest moments.

When you know your purpose,
you move from what you do to why you do it.

Your Definition of Success

Recap

The Foundation for Success

- Come back to the simple things in life, always.

- Check in with who you are.

- Discover what is true, good, and possible about yourself.

- Take note of the lessons you've learned.

- Be aware of your values when making decisions.

- Treasure golden moments daily.

- Be true to your own definition of success.

Reflections

- Celebrate the little things.

- Forgive your past mistakes.

- Be proud of who you are.

- Know your definition of success.

- Be clear on your daily purpose.

- Use your senses to notice the special moments in life.

- Be grateful for what you have in life.

- You can be who you want to be.

Top Tips

- Don't get out of bed in the morning until you have gone through your purpose for the day and taken a deep breath.

- Tap into the feeling of when you were at your best and re-create that feeling in your body before you get up in the morning.

- Remember, you have the power to choose your attitude for the day.

- Write down your values and definition of success and put them where you can see them daily, like on your car dashboard, your vision board, or your bathroom mirror, or set it as a screen saver on your computer.

- Program your values into your smartphone/computer as well.

- Whenever you feel too busy and out of control, go back to the basics. Revisiting your values daily will help you make informed decisions.

- Know your definition of success for the day ahead so that your intentions are clear.

- At the end of each day, think of three amazing things that happened—the treasures of the day.

- Make a pact with yourself to be *you* and no one else.

True success
stems from how
we feel now.

Part 2

Simplify

Beauty of style
and harmony and grace
and good rhythm
depend on simplicity.

Plato, Greek philosopher

Simplify
Your Life

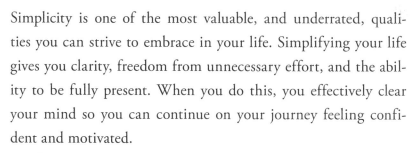

Simplicity is one of the most valuable, and underrated, qualities you can strive to embrace in your life. Simplifying your life gives you clarity, freedom from unnecessary effort, and the ability to be fully present. When you do this, you effectively clear your mind so you can continue on your journey feeling confident and motivated.

After exploring the first section of the book, you now know your values and purpose and when you're at your best. You've also identified the lessons you've already learned, the golden moments that pull you forward, and your definition of success. You've created a foundation for your life.

The next step is to create a structure that will support your success. This means getting back to basics: clearing the clutter, deleting the drainers, and setting some boundaries so that the obstacles we all encounter don't bring your dreams crashing down.

Simplicity Brings Clarity

When you simplify your life, you stop wasting your precious energy. The clarity this brings reduces ambiguity and eliminates doubt. You then have the space and opportunity to set and achieve the goals that matter most to you.

Simplicity represents clarity, presence, and freedom from effort.

Identify
Your Drainers

Is your life full of clutter? We are living in the age of time famine and digital overload, and the expectation to be "on" constantly means there has never been a more important time for you to decompress, declutter, and recalibrate your mind and body to ensure your well-being. Make space to be creative, spontaneous, and free.

High achievers often struggle with feeling cluttered, overwhelmed, and overextended because they take on a lot of commitments. Working parents know only too well how difficult it is to juggle work, life, and play. But really, no one is immune to the burden of being mentally cluttered: the barista at your local café may be chatting politely as he foams your latte, but he's also wondering whether he should move in with his girlfriend, thinking about his plans for the weekend, wondering if he can afford to go to a music festival next month . . . and don't those concert tickets go on sale tomorrow?

Drainers aren't things we think about consciously but are tasks in our subconscious. Decluttering your life helps eliminate them, creating a simpler, more streamlined environment. This is the big clean-out you'll need to do before you can structure the new opportunities and strategies that support you to be your best, with optimal wellness in every part of your life.

Clearing the Drainers

Many people are surprised to realize how much satisfaction they can derive from doing small, seemingly inconsequential tasks, such as putting all their gadget chargers in one place, booking a checkup with the dentist, or filing documents in their correct folders. These types of tasks may not seem like big priorities, but when they are left undone, they can take up mental space and chip away at your everyday focus.

By making small adjustments to your routine, you can create space within your life to manage and create everything you want to achieve. These adjustments can be anything from getting out your clothes for the following day before you go to sleep at night to setting up automatic reminders in your phone to book repeat appointments, like medical checkups and haircuts. Clearing your drainers has a massive positive impact on your energy and your confidence, as you'll experience the satisfaction of accomplishing something—especially if you remember to celebrate all of the wins, big and small, along the way.

Drainers

Drainers are like tiny sandbags that are stacked at the back of your neck. Each sandbag on its own may be small and insignificant, but when they're combined, they weigh you down and make you feel tired, lethargic, stressed, and chaotic. Your personal environment, finances, relationships, and well-being are the key areas where you need to simplify and eliminate drainers.

Your environment says a lot about your state and confidence in life. Clean, open, soul-nourishing space gives your body and mind room to breathe, grow, and maintain perspective. Your surroundings significantly impact your attitudes, experience of life, and happiness and can dictate the base level of stress you may experience each and every day.

Many of us live in a world of "stuffocation" where our identity is defined by our belongings. Simplifying allows you to clear your mind so you can continue on your journey with confidence, free from clutter that may be holding you back. Your body experiences clutter when it is filled with stuck and old thoughts, many of which sabotage your days and goals. Tired, negative beliefs and habits create low-lying weight and stress in your mind and body, which can be detrimental as you strive to grow from year to year.

What Are Your Drainers?

Think about the following aspects of your life—whenever your answer to a question is no, this indicates a drainer. Work to make all your answers yes.

1. Personal Environment

- Is your living space clean and inspiring?

- Is your wardrobe tidy, and are all of your clothes clean, pressed, and in good repair?

- Have you cleaned out your storage space and thrown away anything you haven't used in two years?

- Do you have fresh air and comfort in your home?

- Are your bed, pillow, and bedding clean, comfortable, and conducive to a good night's sleep?

2. Finances

- Do you have a budget or know your cost of living?

- Do you pay your bills on time or make arrangements with creditors?

- Are all of your receipts, invoices, and financial records filed and in order?

- Do you have an automatic savings plan to save at least 10 percent of your income?

- Do you pay off your credit card debt in full each month?

3. Relationships

- Do you tidy any loose ends with your partner, parents, siblings, and friends by having open, honest, and authentic conversations?

- Do you let the people you love know how important they are to you?

- Have you let go of any relationships that drag you down or damage you?

- Do you make requests rather than complaints?

- Do you respond to phone calls, letters, and emails promptly, even if your response is brief?

4. Well-Being

- Does your diet include fresh fruit and vegetables and provide you with enough energy?

- Do you avoid excess tea, coffee, and alcohol?

- Do you exercise for thirty minutes at least three times per week?

- Do you get enough sleep at least five nights a week?

- Do you have a vacation at least once a year?

5. Fun/Creativity

- Do you invest in personal development?

- Do you laugh every day?

- Do you have a hobby?

- Do you plan regular fun activities with your partner, family, and friends?

- Do you dream big dreams and work on realistic ways to make them happen?

Clear the clutter. Get rid of the drainers. Gain fresh and new clarity.

Clear the Clutter

Clutter can make you feel stuck. When it accumulates in your living space, it really has an effect on your state of mind, reminding you of all those things you mean to get around to but somehow never do. They add up in your mind until suddenly there are just too many, and the result is that none of them get done. Clutter makes it hard to relax and feel motivated at home, and it can even affect your social life if you're too embarrassed to have people over.

Quick Clutter Fixes

- Declutter paper—books/magazines/filing.

- Repeat the mantra of one new thing in, one old thing out.

- Clean up one room at a time.

- If you take it off, hang it up.

- If you open it, close it.

- If you use it, clean it.

How to Stay Clutter-Free

- Review your list of drainers monthly.

- Aim to move each answer from no to yes.

- Create a schedule to maintain your personal environment, finances, relationships, and well-being.

- Create a system to achieve all of the tasks you've set yourself to clear the drainers from your life.

- Set aside certain tasks for each week or each month of the year and then do them to keep the drainers from becoming overwhelming.

Do not underestimate the satisfaction that can be derived from doing small, seemingly inconsequential tasks.

Make Technology Work for You

Technology was supposed to make our lives easier, faster, and more efficient. How's that working out for you?

I regularly dedicate some time to thinking about my technology strategy and whether it is working. Is technology causing me stress? Is it robbing me of my time and ability to succeed? Is it affecting my personal relationships and making it harder to renew myself?

Ideally, we should control the flow of information that comes to us, rather than it controlling us. Constant access to technology has been found to deprive us of sleep, health, relationships, space, and our sense of achievement. We are addicted to information delivered at the touch of a button whenever we like, increasingly putting us in the passenger seat of life and distracting us from who we truly are and what our purpose is. When we are tuned in all the time, we lose the ability to really focus on one thing and do it well; we are partially present in life. Is that how you want to live? Having your own plan to make technology work for you is the key to using it to enhance, rather than deplete, the life you want to live.

For instance, having phones on the table during dinner does not improve either the conversation or your sense of connection. Seeing pictures of other people on Facebook or Instagram can decrease your confidence when you consider yourself or your lifestyle in comparison. But setting reminders and alerts so you don't have to remember everything yourself is very useful, as are mindfulness and health apps and downloads that you can listen to on the commute to work, and of course, smartphones make it much easier to stay in touch with people. Think about the way you use technology and make whatever adjustments are necessary to ensure it's to your advantage.

Take Charge of Your Technology

Use your smartphone to help you simplify and declutter your mental space. Do this by programming alerts to take your supplements or medication at the same time each morning and prompts every couple of hours to drink water, stand up, and stretch your legs. Program reminders for things you need to do later in the day, like taking out money to pay your house cleaner, buying milk on the way home after work, or picking up medication on your lunch break. Your phone can keep track of the important tasks and also cover the basics so that you don't have to remember everything.

Quick Tips

- Do not allow phones in the bedroom or at meals.

- When you're out with friends, have a rule that whoever spends time on their phone pays the bill.

- Program your phone/computer to work for you.

- Program your phone not to receive emails from 8:00 PM to 7:00 AM.

- Program it to remind you of your own values.

- Never walk into your home, or your family's or friends' homes, while you're on the phone; finish your conversation before you walk in the door.

- Ensure you have at least one hour of family time each day where all the phones are switched off.

Motivation is what gets you started. Habit is what keeps you going.

Jim Ryun, Olympic medalist

Reset Your Habits

It's estimated we spend up to 40 percent of our day on habits, many of which we don't even know we have. That's a lot of time to waste on unnecessary actions that are not doing anything to move you toward the success you crave.

You can declutter your habits and create the life you want by choosing to develop habits that support your values and who you are. It's important to know that all habits run on a simple loop of:

Cue: Time, person, place, or situation that sets your habit(s) off

Routine: What the habit actually involves

Reward: The payoff for doing it

In order to declutter your habits, first, you need to identify them and recognize the cues that kick them off. Then, think about which habits you would like to stop and ensure you avoid the cues that get them started. To create new, more constructive habits, think about how you spend the first hour of your day and see if you can build those stronger habits into this time. What is your strategy to get going on the right foot each morning? How do you cue up the behavior? What's your routine? What's the payoff?

Habits and attitude determine most of your success.

Make New, Better Habits

Habits are the cornerstone of day-to-day living. For better or worse, your habits shape you, and your life to date is the sum of your habits. A good habit can be a strong ally in your pathway to becoming the person you want to be, while a bad habit can sabotage your best intentions. Mastering your habits to support your vision and purpose will change your life.

Habits are thoughts and behaviors so strongly wired into your mind that you perform them without thinking. They are learned and repeated over time, performed automatically, and persistent, making them hard to break or change. Happy and successful people form habits that feed their success rather than their failure.

They own their habits, work with them, master them, and consistently review them.

To upgrade and master your habits, identify what is and is not working for you, set up your systems, shift your mindset, and find some accountability.

What is a bad habit you would like to change?

_____

_____

What is a good habit you want to replace it with?

_____

_____

What habit do you need to change right now?

_____

_____

What are two decisions you have been putting off that, when you make them now, will change your life?

_____

_____

Some examples of new, better habits could be:

- Make your bed to start your day.

- Move your body before breakfast.

- Meditate for ten minutes a day.

- Drink six to eight cups of water each day and hydrate properly.

- Plan for eight hours of sleep every night.

- Eat whole foods.

- Find gratitude in your day.

Get up and move it: Move your body more often for the physical and mental benefits, not to mention the enjoyment!

Meditate: Take a moment, or ten minutes, if you can, to center yourself every day.

Rehydrate: Avoid the lethargy and inability to concentrate that comes with dehydration. Buy a nice refillable water bottle and take it everywhere with you and keep a large jug of water on your desk at work. Aim for six to eight cups a day.

Refuel: Put wholesome, nutritious energy into your body to avoid the mood swings that come with sugar highs and lows and keep your body functioning at its optimal level.

Think ahead: Prepare yourself for the following day before going to bed.

Things I'd Like to Start Doing on a Regular Basis

1. _____

   _____

2. _____

   _____

3. _____

   _____

4. _____

   _____

5. _____

   _____

6. _____

   _____

7. _____

   _____

8. _____

   _____

9. _____

   _____

10. _____

    _____

Set Your Boundaries

Feeling overwhelmed? Taken on too much? Having trouble saying no? The key to creating a more balanced life is to set boundaries that support your visions, your goals, and the way you function at your best.

Boundaries are set to protect that asset—which is you. Boundaries are essential to becoming a healthy adult and effectively balancing your work and personal life. They demonstrate your commitment to self-respect. Personal boundaries are the physical, emotional, and mental limits we establish to protect ourselves from being manipulated, used, or violated by others and also from sabotaging ourselves. One of the great benefits of setting boundaries is that they will afford you the time, space, and energy to devote yourself to what you are passionate about—your own vision, goals, dreams, and aspirations.

Boundaries provide a valuable structure for communicating with those around you, at work and at play, so that everyone achieves their desired outcome without feeling frustrated or resentful. But first, you need to know where your boundaries are.

So, when should you say no? Cheryl Richardson, author of *The Art of Extreme Self-Care*, suggests you create your own "absolute" list to set boundaries for your optimal life.

What is an absolute yes in your life?

What is an absolute no in your life?

Learning to say no is liberating and brings you back to being true to yourself. Try practicing saying no in the mirror a few times until you sound—and feel—clear, calm, and confident.

Polite Ways to Say No

Many people, especially women, struggle to say no out of fear of sounding rude. But it is a vital skill that stops you from committing to things that drain you and don't add anything positive to your life. Here are some suggestions for polite ways to say no:

- I'm swamped right now, but please ask me again another time. (If you'd like to do it at a later date.)

- I can't do it, but I can recommend someone else.

- I'd love to help, but I'd be letting other people down, and I just can't do that.

- I'm sorry to disappoint you, but I promised myself I would say no to things when I'm feeling overloaded.

EXAMPLE

Boundaries at Work

Mike, a manager of an electronics company, found that if he completed his most important tasks in the morning, he could make himself more available to his colleagues in the afternoon. To achieve this, he always started with the hardest task first. He also set the boundary that when his office door was closed, his colleagues weren't allowed to enter unless their request was urgent, and if it was open, they had to knock before entering.

EXAMPLE

Boundaries at Home

Rosa recognized that her partner and family were the most important people in her life. She decided that between 6:00 PM and 9:00 PM, she would be engaged with them, so she didn't check her phone or emails during this time. She also consciously entered the house each evening with a smile and positive energy, so she would inspire, rather than drain them. Rosa changed her family dynamic with these new simple commitments.

We are only busy with those things we say yes to.

Set boundaries that support your visions and goals and the way you function at your best.

Boundaries for Yourself

By making one basic health commitment to yourself, such as giving up or limiting alcohol or coffee, you can bring about a huge positive change. Jasmin lost eight pounds in six months simply by giving up soft drinks.

_____

_____

_____

_____

_____

_____

Remember a life with boundaries doesn't mean being rigid or inflexible, but having good boundaries creates and cultivates a purposeful life with great meaning and happiness. It allows you to stay in the driver's seat.

- Be in control of your life.

- Be confident in your ability to say no.

- Communicate your thoughts and opinions with calm confidence.

63

Characteristics of Successful People

What sets successful people apart? High achievers have been found to possess certain characteristics that are integral to success. Whatever your goals in life, if you develop the characteristics of an ambitious person, you'll make progress toward your outcomes and have more chance of success.

Consider the experience of elite athletes. They obviously have an innate skill in their chosen sport, but they weren't born performing at an Olympic standard. They worked hard to develop their skills, because they possessed certain characteristics—drive, persistence, passion, determination—that helped them get up at 4:00 AM each day to train for six hours a day, six days a week.

What's Your Opportunity?

Do you have the characteristics of success? Review the following list and see where your approach might need a little fine-tuning to ensure you are doing what you need to create the life you most want to live.

When going through this process with me, Olympic runner Benita Willis realized that although running was her passion, it had taken over her life. She ran too much and had lost her love for it. She had no vision for her life outside of sport, so I helped her build a new routine that supported a full, inspiring, and balanced lifestyle. "I never believed I could achieve so much while being an elite athlete!" she told me. "I feel confident in all areas of my life now and look forward to an exciting future—as an athlete and beyond."

Sometimes the answer to success is identifying the simple characteristic that is needed.

Eleven Characteristics of Successful People

- Having a vision that's complete, inspiring, balanced, and exciting.

- Developing a well-thought-out plan that backs up their vision and also takes their well-being into account.

- Working hard—high-level success starts with the recognition that hard work pays off.

- Having knowledge or training and being committed to adapting and growing continually to improve their skills.

- Supporting an eagerness to learn—winners study, ask questions, read, and research, and then apply what they learn.

- Having persistence—many people give up after their first rejection, but winners look for other opportunities to reach their outcome.

- Taking responsibility—they know that when they blame others for their actions, they disempower themselves.

- Networking—they value people and relationships, and their contact lists are full of people who put a high value on their friendship.

- Making decisions where others procrastinate.

- Demonstrating self-reliance—taking the initiative and accepting the responsibilities of success.

- Living in the present—successful people don't waste time; they use it and complete their tasks mindfully.

Recap

We need to simplify and declutter to regain control of our lives. It is not that hard, but it takes a plan and some action without procrastination.

Drainers occur daily when we let our guard down—the mess comes in, the new purchases arrive, the information never seems to stop. Having your own plan of how to stay decluttered and operate simply and effectively is critical for long-term success.

Simplify for Success

- Get clarity on what drains you physically, mentally, and emotionally.

- Limit the amount of time you spend on electronic devices daily.

- Structure and program technology to work for you and serve you.

- Know your habits. Work with them, change them, and challenge them.

- Set clear and simple boundaries.

- Know when and how to say no, so you have time to do the things that matter the most.

- Be aware of your success characteristics and focus on those that need improving.

Reflections

- Get excited by the fact that less is best.

- Clutter is clog.

- Energy is created by simplifying.

- Love a simple life.

- Change my habits so they work for me.

- Get more organized.

- Boundaries offer support.

- This is my life, and I am the driver.

- Don't think about it; just do it.

- Learn to say no.

- Is technology working for me or against me?

- Tune out sometimes to be fully present in life.

- Hard work pays off.

- Be decisive and persistent.

Top Tips

- Declutter at least one thing each day. For instance, you might start with a wardrobe, then a bookshelf, then an office drawer, and so on.

- Donate old work clothing to a local charity that supplies professional work clothes to the unemployed.

- Tidy up your work desk and keep it as clear as possible.

- Set up your technology so it works for you, not the other way around.

- Program good-habit reminders into your phone.

- Create an automatic debit system to fast-track a savings plan.

- Use tools to limit social media use. There are programs and apps that can block the internet at certain times of the day to give you a break.

- Practice saying no calmly and confidently.

- If you need to say no to someone, write down a polite no statement and practice it out loud so you're clear about what to say, rather than hoping the right thing will come out during the conversation.

- Look at your drainers list and identify the no conversations you need to have, even with yourself (such as, "No thanks, I can't afford it.").

- Start each day with a habit for success.

- Tomorrow starts today. Get yourself organized tonight to be ready for tomorrow morning.

- Be in charge of your boundaries.

- Identify and tidy up the clutter in your life, one step at a time.

- Design boundaries at home to nurture and protect home life and carve out quality time without distractions.

- Design boundaries at work to limit unproductive time, especially meetings and petty gossip.

Simplicity is the ultimate sophistication.

Leonardo da Vinci, Italian artist and scientist

Part 3

Take Control

The grand essentials of happiness are: something to do, something to love, and something to hope for.

George Washington Burnap,
American author and clergyman

Get in the Driver's Seat

It is time to get creative and envision your story for the future. I do this with the help of a vision board, a visual representation of how I'd like my life to look. Every year I redo my vision board and revisit where I am, what I have put my energy into, and what possibilities are next. I update it with new pictures, quotes, and words to focus on, and it is my treasure map to guide my next steps. It gives me purpose, clarity, direction, and confidence. It keeps me motivated and inspired and challenges me to stretch beyond a place of comfort.

The result of this simple practice over the past ten years has been a deepening knowledge of my desires, a greater sense of satisfaction and joy as life unfolds, and a growing sense of achievement. I can comfortably say no, my boundaries are clear, and everything is driven toward my core values. It is my map to fall back on when life takes unexpected twists.

Vision boards are also great fun to put together. Positive images pull us forward into new possibilities that fuel us with hope, put us on the road to finding solutions, and help us realize that we have the power to make things happen in our lives. A clear vision helps you communicate your intentions to yourself and motivates you to start acting accordingly. After all, how are you going to get where you want to go if you have no idea what success actually looks like?

To get in the driver's seat of your life, you need to know where you're heading; without a clear vision, you make yourself life's passenger. This section is about stretching yourself, stirring up your creative side, and mapping your dreams to create the life you most want to live. The goal is to think of exciting possibilities for what could be and to discover the greatest destination for yourself.

Write Your Three-Year Plan

Three years is 156 weeks, 1,095 days, or 1,576,800 minutes. What could you do in that time?

Most of my clients are so busy that they don't have the space to imagine their future, and they lack the tools to explore the potential of their best possible future selves. They're very clear on all the things they don't want, but when I ask them where they would like to be in three years, there are a lot of blank faces. The problem with this approach is that when we don't take control of our own future, life tends to knock us down.

I always start this exercise by writing my age in three years on a piece of paper and then the ages of my family members. Straight away I have something concrete to help me think about what this unfolding picture might look like.

Then I give myself permission to just let go. To let the past be the past for a moment. To put my doubts and worries to one side. To simply dream that if everything went as well as it could, what would my life look like three years from now?

I write down whatever comes to mind, unedited by my fears and unlimited by lack of money, skills, or time. All the hopes and dreams I'm carrying for the next three years of my life are there on the page. Here are some questions to help kick-start your thoughts:

- If you truly lived your purpose each day, what would you be doing that gave your life meaning?

- If you were at your best more frequently, how do you think life would feel?

- If you acted only on your values, what would others say about the way you were living?

- If your definition of success was being realized, what accomplishment would you be proudest of?

- If you were mindful of the golden moments in your life, what would you see?

Get Specific

- What kind of work will you be doing? How do you feel about this work?

- How much money will you be earning? What are you doing with it?

- What's your health like? How are you getting this result?

- Who brings you joy in your life? How do you spend your time together?

- What are you learning? What difference does this make in your life?

- What do you do for fun? Do you have a hobby or a passion project? Are you traveling?

- Where are you living? What makes this feel like a haven?

- What have you conquered emotionally?

- Who are your role models and mentors?

- How are you moving through the world?

If we remove the restrictions we place
on ourselves, we are open to more opportunities.
Dream big if you want to live big.

Jackson's Vision

I'm relaxing at a five-star resort in Thailand with my family, enjoying the fruits of success from a very committed year of work. I'm on a career high after landing a prestigious and lucrative promotion that I've been working toward my entire career, and I feel creatively satisfied in my work. We own a beautiful home on the water, which we're renovating, and we've just settled on our second investment property purchase. We're planning a two-month family adventure around Europe next year. My wife and I enjoy monthly date nights and weekend getaways without the kids every three to four months. I've spent the past couple of years working on my self-development as a person, and I feel happy and content with who I am, both personally and professionally. It's liberating to experience such freedom as a result of planning who I am and where I want to get to.

Luciana's Vision

After working full-time as a hospital nurse for many years, my partner and I have managed to pay off most of our mortgage and our kids are old enough to need less from us, so I've returned to college to pursue a higher degree in an area I've become passionate about—midwifery. I'm only working three days a week at the hospital, so while

I still enjoy the adrenaline rush of a busy shift, I also have more balance in my life. As well as studying, I'm able to take more time to exercise and look after my own health and see more of my partner and children. I do some volunteer work in the community, educating disadvantaged women on looking after their health and caring for their babies, and get a lot of satisfaction from knowing I've contributed positively to their lives. Because I've learned to prioritize myself, I'm able to give energy to others without resenting it.

Creating a vision and purpose is essential.
Without them, you are a passenger in life.

The Grand Adventure

Think of your life as a grand adventure. To get creative, you'll need some space and a blank page or board and permission from yourself to just let go. Start with your mind in a place of abundance. There is such abundance in life that many of us do not see or acknowledge. When you think of all the things you have and what is around you, you are living abundantly. There are flowers, trees, fresh air, and running water—so much to be grateful for. Focusing on what you already have, and the choices you can make, is a great place to start.

How to Create Your Three-Year Plan

- Write down your age and the ages of your family members in three years.

- Put your mind in a place of abundance. Focus on the things you already have and the choices you're free to make.

- Spend fifteen to twenty minutes each day for three days in a row just writing down what you hope your life will be like three years from now.

- Be as specific and detailed as possible, so you can see, feel, and hear what this new reality will be like.

- Notice which ideas you keep coming back to once you've completed this exercise.

Beware of dream stealers: people who encourage you to play it safe and make you believe you'll never reach your dreams.

Create Your Vision Board

How can you start to make your three-year vision a reality? I use a one-year vision board as a means of turning my longer-term dreams into shorter-term realities. It helps me paint a picture of the future I want to achieve, providing a daily touchpoint to inspire and guide me.

For example, if you want to be healthier, an image of the type of food you want to be eating will remind you of this each day. When you can see things, you can start feeling them, and then you can start believing in them and setting up the structures to get you there.

Creativity and visualization are life skills that can be practiced. Remember, like attracts like. Whatever we focus on, we give energy to. If we focus on stress, we get more stress. If we want joy, we need to feel and acknowledge joy when it is there; if we want well-being, we need to feel and focus on well-being. What are you envisioning for the upcoming year?

Start by simply printing out pictures or cutting from magazines images or words that inspire you. Look through books for words, quotes, and affirmations that warm your heart. Think in key themes—like career, family, health, finance, fun, and home—of the kind of life you wrote about creating. The more you can see, hear, and feel what this vision of your future will be like, the stronger the pull to make it your reality will be. Pictures, words, symbols, and colors are a great way to start tangibly creating this new reality.

There are also digital options for creating vision boards you might consider if you want to see yours on your smartphone or as a screen saver. Whatever process you choose, be sure you can see your vision daily to guide you forward.

Let your vision board be your gift, your light, and your constant reminder of how you want to grow and evolve.

Questions to Ask as You Make Your Vision Board

- Where will you be living a year from now?

- What will you be doing for work a year from now?

- Who will you be with a year from now?

- What emotions will you be feeling in a year?

- How will you look after your health in a year?

- Who will be inspiring your journey in a year?

- What will you be learning a year from now?

- What are you telling yourself with these pictures?

- Is this the life you most want to be living?

How active is your vision board? This is your destiny, so make it vivid, vibrant, and vital. Make it count.

Once you have completed your board, hang it in a spot where you can see it daily. Mine is in my office; some people hang theirs behind their bedroom door so they wake up to it. When you see it often, you start to commit it to memory; it becomes a part of your destiny and meditation process. Let your subconscious mind continually absorb this new reality every day and night, reminding you where you are heading in life. Allow the opportunities to flow into your life, and because you know where you want to go, you will see them clearly.

My vision board represents the space I need in life, the well-being that is at my foundation, my relationships, my role models, and the characteristics in myself that I want to develop, my house/car and other belongings, and the places I want to travel. It includes my hobbies and the emotions I want to feel, as well as the basic things I am grateful for in life. It represents my purpose, values, and definition of success. It gives me the confidence, optimism, and courage to create the life I most want to be living.

Success is when I approve of myself and what I am doing each day.

Stretch Yourself

What was the last new thing you learned? We are creatures of progress, with a lifetime of hunger for improvement. The very fact that we continue to evolve over the course of our lives is evidence of our ongoing need for growth and learning.

Yet as we get older, the chance to discover new approaches, new ideas, and new wonders often fades away in the everyday business of life. But without opportunities to stretch ourselves, we soon stagnate and plateau into lives of boredom and disappointment. So, what are you learning?

I find that I learn best by listening, so I'm a big fan of audiobooks and podcasts. Truth is, it doesn't matter what form your learning takes, whether it's reading books, attending a formal course or public lecture, taking part in a conversation, or observing an informal life lesson. The point is simply to seek opportunities that stretch you just beyond your comfort zone and offer new challenges that help you grow.

That's right: it's not enough just to absorb information—we actually need to apply what we learn to our lives to enjoy the true value of our discoveries. One of the easiest ways to do this is to think about the questions that new insights might prompt us to ask about the lives we're living.

Seek out challenges that stretch you just beyond your
comfort zone and offer new opportunities for growth.

How Could I Experiment with This Idea in My Life?

Here are some of my favorite questions to fire up my brain and get me stretching a little further:

- If there was one thing I could do based on what I've just learned, what would it be?

- If I lived my life by this lesson, where would I be three years from now? Is this what I want?

- How might this lesson have an impact on my vision for the year ahead?

- If there was no chance of failure, what things would I be willing to try?

- What would it take to master this part of life? Am I up for it?

- Where can I learn more about this idea? Who could I talk to about it?

Going Further

Here are some more questions I like to ask myself to stretch my life vision further when I feel things have become too comfortable:

- If I were to fully live my life and feel a holistic sense of well-being, what could I do right now?

- How would I feel about adding five daring goals that really would be a stretch?

- How can I be more specific in each area of my life?

- What makes my heart sing?

- If I had all the money and success that I desire, what would I do with it?

Map Your Goals
and Dreams

Now that you know where your life is headed in the longer term (your three-year vision) and the shorter term (your one-year vision board) and the places you might be able to stretch yourself, it's time to figure out how you'll get from where you are to where you want to go. Yes, it's time for a little reality check to see what goals you're really willing to set.

You see, while most of us believe tomorrow could be better than today, only half of us believe we can actually make it so. And this is the difference between wishing for the future we want to create and hoping for it. To have hope, we need some clear want-to (rather than have-to) goals, pathways to move us toward these goals, and a plan to maintain our willpower to get us to the final result.

Hope is the work of your head and your heart. Not only does it lift your spirits, it also buoys your energy, makes life worthwhile, and changes your day-to-day behavior. So, what are you hoping for?

Start by identifying three to five goals you want to accomplish this year. I start by looking at my vision board and noting some specific goals for the year ahead.

Five Steps to Clarify Your Goals

- What are your goals in simple terms?

- Are you clear on your specific objectives?

- Why are you doing this?

- What do you really want to achieve?

- Do your goals have depth and do you really understand them?

Rather than thinking, "I'll be more healthy, both physically and mentally," be more specific: "I'll do yoga at least three times a week, meditate before bed at least three times a week, and make sure every meal contains fresh produce." Make sure the goals you set are achievable, as there's no point in setting unrealistic goals destined for failure.

Then, try to find at least three pathways—actions you can take—to make these goals a reality. This could be booking yourself into a yoga course, putting a reminder note on your bedside table to meditate before going to sleep, and spending half an hour on Sundays to plan the food you are going to eat over the coming week. I try to think about what I'll do each day, each week, and each month to start getting the outcome I want. Again, try to be as specific as possible; so, rather than thinking, "Get more training," try, "Complete a short course learning leadership techniques."

Next, think of at least one obstacle that may arise for each of your pathways. Perhaps working late and last-minute social occasions could disrupt your yoga. Studies have found we're more likely to reach our goals if we plan for the obstacles up front, so be honest about what might slow you down, trip you up, or make you give up completely.

Finally, write down all the things you can do to maintain your willpower as you set about making your goals a reality. How will you make the journey enjoyable? Is there someone, a friend, work colleague, or family member, who can support you along the way? How will you measure your progress? What will you do to celebrate the small milestones? These details will be vital for helping you achieve the outcomes you desire.

Make Your Dreams a Reality

- Carry them with you all day.

- Write them on your bathroom mirror in fluorescent text.

- Put them alongside your vision board.

- Program them into your phone.

- Write them on a card and store it in your wallet.

- Copy them onto the front page of your planner so they greet you when you open it each day.

EXAMPLE

Rachell's Dreams

My client Rachell was hoping to take a break from her job. A senior IT specialist, she was unhappy with the culture of the office and lack of opportunities for women. Her goal was straightforward: resign gracefully and identify a new role with a similar salary of $250,000. She was doing this to open up her career to the next chapter, capitalize on her expertise in big data and artificial intelligence, and ensure that her career was not inhibited by outdated ideas about women in IT. The pathway she needed to take was to create a new résumé, let her network know she was interested in a new role, and begin conversations with headhunters.

She broke down the tasks into little wins and successfully moved through the tasks. Her biggest fear was not being "a contender"; however, she received four job offers within three weeks. The process also allowed her to see her professional value in a new light.

EXAMPLE

Jana's Big Change

After thirty years of marriage, Jana needed to make a major change. She and her husband had separated on three occasions, but Jana had always come back, wanting to keep her family together. Now, with her youngest child being twenty-three, Jana decided that it was time. Her goals centered around a smooth transition to her new life, supporting the family unit to adjust to the separation, and building a new life for herself. She broke these goals down into a range of tasks to ensure that the process was able to go smoothly: blocking off time to manage financial affairs, making time for self-care and counselling, planning time with each of her three children, and beginning a dream goal of getting back to dance classes.

Do your goals have depth, and do you really understand them?

My Tip

When setting your goals, start with your overall vision, including those big dreams and lofty pie-in-the-sky ambitions. This will help you break them down into smaller wins, with each step taking you closer to your final goal. I write down my intention and affirmation for each day in the morning, so I really focus and get that sense of achievement; no matter how small the task is, it is on track with my vision.

We're more likely to reach our goals if we plan for the obstacles up front, so be honest about what might slow you down, trip you up, or make you give up completely.

If you don't have time to write down your goals, when are you going to find the time to accomplish them?

Example Dream Map

TOPIC	GOAL	OBSTACLE
Mental Health	Have 1 hour a day of space.	No time, too busy
Physical Health	Eat breakfast.	Always in a rush, too tired, can't be bothered
Relationships	Be honest and open, supportive and generous.	Honesty can be painful at times, lack of time and energy to invest in people
Finances	Pay off credit card debt.	Lack of money
Personal Environment	Stay tidy for clarity.	Lack of time, task is overwhelming
Career	Get more clients.	Too busy to spend time looking for them
Passions/ Hobbies	Have more fun in life.	Too busy, too tired

PATHWAY	OUTCOME
30 minutes of morning meditation—get up earlier. Silence in the car. Phone ban of 1 hour when I arrive home.	Feeling of space and control in my life. Having a simple, defined rule makes it easy to achieve.
Prepare food the night before. Make it delicious so it'll be worth the effort.	More energy in the morning. Not as likely to eat unhealthy morning snacks.
Focus on who I want to be in the relationship. Stop comparing myself to others. Stay away from drainers and dream stealers.	Feel energetic and enjoy people. Attract more like-minded people when I am focusing on being the best me I can be.
Start a cost-of-living spreadsheet to record what I spend money on. Put a hold on my credit card.	Regain control of my money. Can make more informed choices that add to my confidence, rather than spending for therapy!
One-touch rule. Don't shuffle things around; put them away. When getting changed, put clothes away.	Less tidying all the time by doing the simple things as they arise and not double-handling everything.
Make one extra call per week. Have a list ready to go that inspires you and keeps you aware of what the reward for your commitment will be.	Get results by making more connections and opening more doors.
Get a friend to be a hobby buddy and try three new things, such as photography, cooking, or a fun run.	Enjoy new options without feeling intimidated and discover new skills to get passionate about.

Your Dream Map

TOPIC	GOAL	OBSTACLE
Mental Health		
Physical Health		
Relationships		
Finances		
Personal Environment		
Career		
Passions/ Hobbies		

PATHWAY	OUTCOME

Recap

As you travel toward your vision, keep a daily journal that helps you celebrate and be grateful for the progress, big and small, that you're making each day. This simple discipline has been found to give us the energy and optimism to keep moving toward our goals.

This is one of the areas I spend a lot of time on in my life. Thinking about my vision, how I'm stretching myself, the hopes I'm focused on achieving, and my sense of gratitude is how I create the incredible life I'm living. It is creative, it is fun, and it keeps me focused on being me. It also helps me stay active, inspired, motivated, and focused on putting energy into the things I really want for my life.

Reflections

- Live your life on purpose.

- Visualize the feelings, thoughts, and things that you want in life.

- Allow yourself to dream.

- Enjoy being creative.

- Love the "now" and the process of creation.

- What you focus on increases.

- Create bite-size tasks that put you in the direction of your vision.

- Always have a daily list of goals and intentions so you stay on track.

- You are your own best friend.

Top Tips

- Create your vision based on your own core values.

- Decide that this is your life and you own it.

- Think three years down the track and plant seeds that will bear fruit.

- Be clear on your vision for the next twelve months and what you want to accomplish.

- Seek sources of learning and ask questions that stretch your thinking.

- Map your hopes and act accordingly.

- When you see an inspiring image or a real-life moment that really reflects who you want to be, capture it on your smartphone and add it to your vision board. Start a collection. It really will come in handy.

- Be specific about something you want to learn—how to do a headstand, master your phobia of public speaking, or speak a foreign language—and then map out a specific plan to get those skills.

- Each day, program reminders into your smartphone that include actions you need to take to achieve goals, like run ten miles in preparation for the half-marathon, transfer $100 to your credit card to stay on target for eliminating debt, or organize a date night for next Saturday.

- Remember to keep tasks bite-size! Break them down so you can make smart, steady progress.

- Keep your vision board and goals visible. A plan that gets filed away will be forgotten with the endless distractions of day-to-day life.

- Think about the dream stealers in your life. Who are they, and how will you limit their negative impact on your life plans? How do you want to deal with them?

- Practice gratitude—find ways to add gratitude into the everyday. Create habits for moments when you'll consciously identify what you are grateful for. This could be while you're waiting at traffic lights, as you sip your first cup of coffee for the day, as you begin a workout, or while tucking your children in at night.

If you want to build a ship, don't drum up people to collect wood and don't assign them tasks and work, but rather teach them to long for the endless immensity of the sea.

Antoine de Saint-Exupéry, French writer

Part 4

Get
Going

The time which we have at
our disposal every day is
elastic; the passions that we
feel expand it, those that we
inspire contract it; and habit
fills up what remains.

Marcel Proust, French writer

Create Your Structure

It is exciting to start this part of the journey, and I suggest that you keep revisiting this chapter. This is the building part, the part that creates the structure to support the purpose, values, and definition of success you have set so that you can make your vision a reality, keep stretching yourself, and realize your hopes. This is where the accomplishments start to kick in and where the rewards begin to pile up.

Structure also gives you easy levers to pull each month to adjust your path as needed. The circumstances of our lives are constantly evolving and our thoughts, feelings, and behaviors sometimes need to shift accordingly. Structure should always guide you but never govern you. It should help you find the rhythm of the life you want to be living.

You're probably already pretty good at creating structures for your life, but I'll hazard a guess that while your annual holiday plans are analyzed, reviewed, and shared in big, bold letters on your calendar, the same attention to structure isn't present in the rest of your life. In my experience, most of us spend more time planning our holidays than we do our health, finances, careers, or families. Of course, there's nothing wrong with looking forward to a vacation, but if it becomes all we really have to live for each year, there's a problem!

Master Your Time

It's important to value time and to understand what it is doing for you—not just when you're taking a break but in every moment. The way you structure your activities either will give you a sense of energy, achievement, success, and fulfillment or will make you feel stressed, out of control, and exhausted.

Time is a gift, and it is our responsibility to "own and drive" it. This means taking responsibility for what we want to feel (unhurried, calm, and relaxed or rushed, anxious, and stressed?) and understanding the consequences of each of our activities.

Our perception of time changes according to our circumstances. Any woman in the throes of labor will tell you that one minute is a very long time. Consider how a fifteen-minute block of time feels when you're in the following situations:

- On a freeway in bumper-to-bumper traffic, with no music and no passengers

- Running late for an appointment or meeting

- In a slow-moving line at the bank, post office, or supermarket

- Waiting for someone who is running late for an appointment with you

- Sipping cocktails on a relaxing vacation

- Deeply immersed in reading a book, watching a film, or doing your favorite hobby

Do You Need More Time?

Are you experiencing a "time famine"—the feeling that you'll never have enough time, no matter how fast you're running? Does this sound familiar to you?

Leslie Perlow of Harvard Business School is a specialist in organizational behavior. Her research indicates that feeling as though we're experiencing a time famine has very real consequences, from increased stress to diminished satisfaction with our lives. But unfortunately, we're often too busy taking action to really think through the importance of what we're doing.

The good news is that we can also create a situation where we feel "time affluent," with all the time we need entirely within our reach. All it takes is the willingness to structure our time around doing the things that really matter and letting go of the idea that our level of busyness somehow defines our level of importance.

Let's change our thinking and embrace planning to focus on the activities that truly make a difference, so we can create the kind of freedom we long for in our lives. Our mantra is, "I have enough time to fulfill all of my dreams."

Structure = Balance and Control = Freedom

Start
Your Planning

Now you have your goals and wish list mapped out, what will the month ahead look like? Start your planning by writing down a list of what you need to do. You might like to use colored pens, colored paper, or a new diary or smartphone app—be creative and make it special so that the very idea of planning feels more exciting and enjoyable. As the month progresses and you make your way through the list, tick things off or cross them out because this gives your brain a lovely hit of dopamine, one of the feel-good chemicals our bodies produce that will help you increasingly look forward to making plans and carrying them out.

Quick Tips to Get Started

- Invest in a diary or smartphone app that gives you annual, monthly, and weekly views of your priorities.

- Make sure your diary or app is something you love and will be excited about using.

- Play around with the diary or app to find the way it works best for you.

- Make this diary or app your touchstone throughout the day to guide what you do.

- Give yourself the pleasure of crossing things off!

Structure is a powerful and highly underrated tool that will fundamentally change your life for the better.

Make a Loose Plan

The world's most effective leaders understand that forward planning is essential for success. By loosely planning each year in advance, month by month, you'll be well prepared for the busy times but also able to factor in plenty of fun.

An annual calendar puts you in charge of how you use your time. It gives you the perspective and focus you need to move from the passenger seat to the driver's side of life. It's the next step in bringing your purpose, vision, and hope map to life.

Four Steps to Plan Your Year

Start with the obvious and jot down birthdays, holidays, and other regular significant events that are part of the rhythm of your life. Don't get bogged down in small details yet—focus on the big-ticket occasions that shape your year.

Add your goal: Looking at your goal map, are there key milestones, events, or opportunities you want to note? For example, the date of the marathon you want to run, a conference you want to attend, or the go-live date of a major project.

Bust the energy drainers: Add any known energy drainers that will have to be taken care of, so you're prepared to tackle these head-on. For example, when will you do your annual tax return, service the car, spring-clean your living space?

Prioritize some fun: Plan some pick-me-ups in your calendar to keep your motivation and energy levels up. For example, have you booked an annual getaway, is there a concert you want to see, would you value a spa day with a friend?

Breathe: Take a deep breath and relax, knowing this list is there to guide you, not govern you, as you focus on the things you most want to complete.

Of course, if your annual calendar looks overwhelming at this point, now is a good time to see what you can delegate, what you can delay until next year, or what you can simply delete. Be sure that when you look at the big picture of what will unfold this year, it is taking you toward the kind of success you want.

Think of this as your road map for life. You're eliminating the dead ends and wrong turns and taking the fastest, most direct route to your destination.

Learn Power Planning

Personal fulfillment depends on how you value each and every moment. Power planning is the key. Now that you have planned your year, as each month approaches, it's time to get more specific about what you want to achieve, the time you need to unwind, and the golden moments you want to create. To create your monthly plan (see page 120), first write down in your annual planner the key activities that occur in the coming month. Now, add:

Personal priorities: Book in personal time in the same way you would schedule a meeting. For example, my family's first hour at home each evening is our most important meeting of the day. Do you need to plan time with your family, your partner, or your friends?

Health and well-being: Exercise, food, fun, and time out are vital and should be shaped around your work.

Hopes: What do you need to focus on doing this month so that you can move forward on your path?

Energy drainers: What are the drainers you need to take care of this month? Dentist, pulling weeds in the yard, paying the bills?

Mental breathing space: Make time for rest and recovery, when you can just hang out and be. I love my couch nights!

When you've finished drawing up your plan for the month, step back and take a look at the big picture once again. Is this the kind of month you want to be living? Is it moving you toward your purpose, vision, and hopes? Are you looking forward to the month unfolding? If the answer is no to any of these, put yourself in the driver's seat and find a way to change the direction, shift gears, or make the journey more enjoyable. This is your life; you need to make conscious choices about the way you live to achieve the outcomes you most desire.

Seeing a month mapped out in advance is liberating and keeps us focused and inspired. Here is an example of a template my clients use to help them plan each month.

SAMPLE MONTHLY PLAN

Health and Well-Being	• Exercise, including when I run, lift weights, stretch, go to yoga • Massages and listening to inspirational and interesting downloads
Personal Priorities	• Date nights, time with the kids, time with extended family, and some fun time and dinners with friends
Hopes	• The outcomes I want to achieve and progress I'd like to make at work • The personal goals I am working toward

YOUR MONTHLY PLAN

Key Activities	
Personal Priorities	
Health and Well-Being	
Hopes	
Energy Drainers	
Mental Breathing Space	

Position It

Looking at your monthly plan, you might be wondering how you'll fit everything in. After all, there are only twenty-four hours in a day, and yet there's so much living to be done.

The good news, as we discovered earlier, is that studies have found most of us spend almost half our day in a haze of habits we may not even be fully aware of. I'm not suggesting you try to claw back all that time, but what if you could be more mindful about how your habits are playing out and use the simple habit loop we discovered earlier of cue, routine, and reward to prioritize some of the changes you want most?

Creating a Weekly Habit Map

The best place to start is by creating a map of your week and noting the key success habits you already have. For example, do you already have an exercise routine, do you have a regular meditation time, do you spend time with your family each evening, and so on? What are the habits that already exist in your week to bring your purpose, values, vision, and hopes to life? And when do they happen? Write these on your weekly map.

Are there other habits you'd like to add to make your most desired behaviors a sure thing? These don't have to be big investments of energy or time; you'll be amazed at what you can accomplish in as little as ten minutes. For example, if one of your hopes is to spend more time catching up with friends, a ten-minute habit of calling or writing to someone first thing each night after dinner can have you touching base with up to thirty people each month. Or if one of your hopes is to learn more about a new topic, a ten-minute habit of reading a book or article each morning before you turn on your computer at work can have you quickly gaining more knowledge. What are the small habits you'd like to create in your week to start prioritizing the changes you want to see in your life? When will these habits take place, and how can you get started? How will you celebrate what you've done so that you'll want to do it again tomorrow? Add these to your weekly map.

Pay particular attention to your morning and evening routines—you want to start the day with power and finish with a good night's sleep.

Make weekly diary planning a habit so you can keep moving toward the outcomes you want. At each weekly update, tick off the things you've achieved—this gives you a sense of accomplishment and boosts your confidence.

Will these habits stick? Are they realistic? Do they fit in with your work hours and your family commitments? Will you still have time for rest and recovery?

Don't set yourself up for failure. Start with small changes, just one at a time, and when a habit begins to stick, add the next one. And then the next one. And then the next one, until you feel that your weeks are truly being spent in the ways you find most rewarding.

It is important to value time and to understand what
it is doing for you—not just when you are taking a break
but at each and every moment.

Write It Down

One of the commitments I urge all my clients to make is to keep a daily diary. This is the moment when all the annual, monthly, and weekly habit plans come together into one clear set of daily action in your daily planner.

Not having a diary is an act of self-sabotage—it's like charging expenses on your credit card all month, not keeping tabs on your spending, never asking for receipts, and then complaining about how high your credit card bill is.

While many people have moved to electronic diaries in recent years, I've found lots of my clients are switching back to paper options. The old saying "don't think it; ink it" seems to be more important than ever. Personally, I don't think it matters which approach you use as long as you are driving it, it is working for you, and you are getting the results and sense of satisfaction you need to stay motivated.

At the start of each week, use your monthly planner and weekly habit map to complete your daily diary. Be sure to note:

- Significant moments and milestones

- Meetings for work, home, or play (with time for travel if required)

- Times for your habits

- Key actions you need to take to help fulfill your hopes

- Energy drainers you need to take care of

Be generous in your allocation of time so you're not running from one activity to the next and driving yourself crazy. And remember the 80/20 rule. Life moves constantly; a reasonable balance to aim for is knowing that you can probably control 80 percent of your time, while 20 percent of the time you'll be thrown a curveball. Leave space for the curveballs so they don't send you into chaos and overwhelm you.

Ask Yourself
Quality Questions

1. Will I feel that this was a day I lived well?

2. Will this move me toward my purpose, vision, values, and hopes?

3. Have I made quality time for the people who are most important to me?

4. What are the rewards and consequences?

5. Have I structured calm and balance into my life by using my success toolkit?

*Depth and fulfillment in life depend on how
you value each and every moment.*

Not having a diary is an act of self-sabotage.

Get Started

My favorite book is *Eat That Frog!* by Brian Tracy. I've found it to be extremely practical when it comes to getting things done. The concept is that the frog is the biggest and most important task of the day, the one you usually procrastinate on. So, to start the day, you discipline yourself to "eat the frog" and do this task immediately, completing it before moving on to anything else. "Eat the frog" is my morning motto and is programmed into my phone.

Self-managing means setting yourself a structure to carry out tasks, such as "eat the frog." People often find it easy to plan, but they have to carry it through by executing the new habits they need to put in place and finishing what they set out to do. Brian Tracy says there are three Ds to address when forming new habits: decision, discipline, and determination. When I'm trying to create new habits to assist with my self-managing, I find it helps to visualize myself as the person I intend to be and that the job is done.

As you can imagine, I have a list a mile long of dreams, ideas, and things to do and a business and family to run. Part of my self-managing is realizing that there needs to be an underlying aim of total well-being for myself. I find that if I am fit, healthy, and well and have had enough sleep and nutritious food, I can ensure my family, my business, and everybody else are getting the best from me.

EXAMPLE

Sangeeta's Frog

For Sangeeta, a writer and Airbnb operator, daily exercise, proper nutrition, and hydration have always been a struggle. With the onset of menopause, a further fifteen pounds added to her weight was making her miserable. Through her daily and weekly habit maps, we looked at ways to truly embed better habits, challenging her defensive mindset that "I know what to do, and I know all about nutrition; it's just my hormones." Essential new daily habits that we made nonnegotiable include: drink one liter of filtered water each morning; replace a heavy cooked breakfast with a light chia pudding; and start each day with four thousand steps, gradually building up to ten thousand steps. We programmed these tasks into her phone for daily reminders. Once a week, she chose Zumba, a high-intensity dance class, as something she was open to doing. No more excuses.

Lindsay's Frog

Lindsay has always chosen extreme working hours, at the expense of her husband and home life. When we were designing her new life plan, we factored into her working week time to watch classic movies with her husband, blocked off full days per week with no screen time, and also planned a ten-day retreat to work on a new project at their upstate farm. This process and answering questions like "Have I made time for the people who are important to me?" made it very clear that she was not managing her work/life balance effectively. Lindsay found the exercise truly valuable, realizing that she needed to challenge and change her habits, show the people she loved that they matter, and be more accountable for her time.

I build my self-motivation through confidence,
positive thinking, focus, and a motivating environment.

Boost Your Motivation

Wanting to do something and actually doing it can be two very different things. The distinction between people who never reach their goals and those who achieve one goal after another often comes down to the ability to self-motivate. Motivation is your internal drive to achieve, produce, develop, evolve, and keep moving toward your goals.

Motivation is linked to your level of initiative in setting challenging goals for yourself and your belief that you have the skills and abilities required to achieve these goals. You can boost your motivation in the following ways:

Confidence: This makes you resilient and driven, viewing difficult goals as challenging rather than impossible. You're more likely to bounce back from setbacks and believe in your ability to succeed.

Realistic optimism: This is particularly important when things aren't going as planned or unexpected setbacks arise. Don't think, "I knew I couldn't do it," but, "This one failure isn't going to stop me."

Focus: Setting clear, strong goals helps you stay focused, as does recognizing your achievements.

Support: Surround yourself with people who remind you of your goals and encourage your progress and are willing to celebrate your success. Seek out resources that will support you.

Your Dream Team

Identifying your dream team and keeping these people around you is an important part of your toolkit and structure for success. Your dream team may include:

- Role models

- Mentors

- Friends

- Coaches

- Personal trainers

- Family

- Colleagues

- Your own mastermind group of like-minded people

- An exercise buddy

You can also find motivation in different tools, such as:

- Books and audiobooks

- Magazines

- Music

- Podcasts

- Public talks (such as TED talks)

- Gratitude journals

Plan your dream team into your life. For example, whenever I go for a walk on my own, I listen to an inspirational audiobook. I set up a monthly coffee date with my mastermind group, see my life coach once a month, and go walking with my fitness buddy once a week. Every night I alternate between writing a gratitude journal entry and listening to a meditation in bed.

What we think,
or what we know,
or what we believe, is
of little consequence.
The only consequence
is what we do.

John Ruskin, English writer

Empower Yourself

When you believe in yourself and you are truly committed to your goals, you will achieve them. When you don't achieve them, the problem is that your level of commitment isn't high enough. In every moment of your life, you are committed to something—you may be lying on the couch watching television, thinking you're not committed to anything, but lying on the couch and watching television is exactly what you are committed to doing.

Our commitment to something can be influenced by an even stronger underlying commitment. These can have both a positive and a negative face. For example, being independent can be a wonderful thing, but it can also be a hindrance in some aspects of your life. Working out an optimal balance is about identifying what you are truly committed to. Following through on commitments is very powerful, as it builds your confidence and builds trust with those around you.

Think of each task on your to-do list or in your diary and consider where it fits on your scale of commitment. Has it been sitting there for months, waiting for you to "find the time"? Which of these levels of commitment are you operating at?

- Hmm . . .

- I'll think about it.

- I'll do it (unless something else comes up).

- I'll do it (unless something important comes up).

- I'll drag myself there bloodied and broken if I have to.

For example, if Martin says, "I'll try to quit smoking this weekend," he really means that he is not ready to commit to quitting and hasn't fully explored the commitments that smoking fulfills. By using the word *try*, he can avoid quitting and exploring what his commitment to smoking actually means. This is a world away from "I will stop smoking on Saturday."

If you're lacking the commitment to follow through on your plans, try this to find the real reasons you're getting stuck:

Write down a goal you've been unable to attain. For example: "Go to the gym twice a week."

Make a list of the actions you have taken (or not taken) that are in direct opposition to this goal. For example: "Worked longer hours, so I told myself I didn't have time; stopped working out with my gym buddy and lost that accountability; eventually canceled gym membership as I wasn't using it."

Imagine that these choices, which have taken you away from your desired goal, are an expression of a deeper commitment. Consider: "What commitment are these choices in direct alignment with?" The underlying commitment is: "My gym membership is expensive, and I'm not getting value, so I'll cancel it and save money."

Now that you know the real reason why this underlying commitment has held you back, reset your goal and truly commit to it. For example, join a gym that offers better value and classes you really like; find cheaper or free ways to exercise such as cycling to work, walking in the park, or doing yoga DVDs at home; or find a friend to work out with and re-establish motivation and accountability.

Every time you just try, instead of truly committing to achieving a set task, you rob yourself of time and energy (both physical and emotional).

Take Responsibility

When you hear the word *responsibility*, do you associate it with a burden to carry or the opportunity to feel free?

When things don't go to plan, we often look for someone to blame, turning ourselves into victims who are resentful and powerless. When you choose to blame, you choose to burden.

But when we take responsibility for the way that our own thoughts, feelings, and behaviors have contributed to a situation, it puts us back in the driver's seat and gives us the power and freedom to respond differently. If you accept the saying, "If it's to be, it's up to me!" there's very little you can't achieve.

Blame burdens us with disempowerment and loss of freedom.

Responsibility frees us with power and choices.

Taking responsibility simply requires us to ask: "What have I done to cause or affect this? What can I do now to improve the situation?"

Consider Lesley, a finance broker who, at the age of fifty-five, lost money in share investments. He was angry. He felt cheated. A large proportion of his life savings was gone, and he blamed his financial advisor for giving him bad advice. He was becoming very bitter over the whole ordeal, which was holding him back from setting new financial goals for his retirement. But he'd agreed to make the investment, which was a gamble, and he needed to take responsibility for his choices.

As well as being disempowering, to blame is to dwell, and hence a waste of time. And blaming yourself is just as damaging as blaming others. Instead, try to think of it as taking responsibility for the things you are responsible for and letting go of the rest. Once you

are ready to do this, you can forgive yourself
or others for mistakes and move on.

Three Steps to
Get Your Life Moving

Blame   *Three things I blame myself or others for:*

Causes   *How did I cause or contribute to the situation?*

Resolution   *How can I take responsibility and improve the situation?*

Choose to blame

=

Choose to burden

Conquer
Self-Sabotage

Does fear, anxiety, or worry ever get the better of your plans? You know those moments, when you unexpectedly find yourself cleaning the house, hiding on the couch, or distracted by 101 other things, none of which your day planner suggests you're meant to be doing right now. All of us suffer occasionally by letting our best intentions be hijacked by fear.

Common Self-Sabotages

- Fear of success

- Fear of failure

- Beliefs such as "I'm not good enough" or "there isn't enough to go around"

- Beliefs such as "I'm independent—I don't need help"

- Beliefs such as "I don't deserve it"

If your fears are holding you back from following through on your purpose, vision, and goals, it is time to recognize that these beliefs are simply stories we tell ourselves. Your brain is a sense-making machine, and one of the ways it puts the pieces of your life together is by constantly creating stories about why things are happening and what might happen next. Sometimes these stories are accurate, but much of the time they're not. When fear is putting you in life's passenger seat, it is time to ask: "Is there any other explanation for what's unfolding?"

Here are some ways to stop self-sabotage:

- Understand your personal self-sabotaging behaviors.

- Identify the root causes.

- Take time for some self-reflection.

- Don't listen to your negative inner critic.

- Find your inner positive voice.

- Stop comparing yourself to others.

- Practice self-compassion.

- Change your pattern of behavior.

- Create small meaningful changes.

- Set goals around them and make plans.

- Start a gratitude journal.

Own your limiting beliefs and work to reduce them.

Prepare for the Obstacles

When you created your goal map, you discovered the importance of planning for obstacles if you want to reach your outcomes. Common obstacles to well-being and success are:

- Not enough time

- Not enough money

- Don't like exercise

- It's too hard

- The timing's not right

- I wouldn't know where to start

- I travel too much

- I don't know the right people

- My family and friends would laugh

- I'm no good at that

- I'm too tired

- If I succeed, people will expect me to keep it up

To ensure these obstacles don't hold you back, challenge yourself to find small changes that make the outcomes you want possible.

If you are fully present with your senses, you can really live life with depth, clarity, and a sense of total abundance.

Prepare to Adapt

Think about the obstacles that may prevent you reaching your goals and how you can plan ahead to overcome them.

Obstacle	Solution
Example: *Not enough time*	• Wake up half an hour earlier and get moving. • Leave work on time, by 6:00 PM. • Work smarter instead of harder.
Example: *Too busy to cook* *healthy meals*	• On Sunday, prepare meals for the week ahead. • Prepare your breakfast ingredients the night before. • Start your own recipe book of healthy, quick meals.

Recap

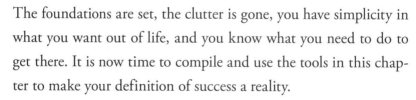

The foundations are set, the clutter is gone, you have simplicity in what you want out of life, and you know what you need to do to get there. It is now time to compile and use the tools in this chapter to make your definition of success a reality.

Creating routine and structure in your day is the key to a calm, balanced, and successful life. Structure is a powerful tool that will fundamentally change your life for the better and give you the kind of time affluence you've only dreamed of.

To achieve your goals, the things that matter most in your life need to be planned and supported: health, relationships, work, money, fun, and time out.

When the right structure is in place, the basics are covered, so you can be spontaneous and grab new opportunities without sacrificing your normal obligations. It gives you balance and clarity and the space and freedom you need to live a life you love. Hold these plans lightly and be guided, but not governed, by the changes you're creating.

Planning my diary annually, monthly, weekly, and daily so that I can drive my habits, tackle difficult tasks, and use technology to support me is the only way I can maintain my energy at an optimal level. Structure is how I ensure I have time for creativity and fun, for self-care and a good night's sleep. It allows me to stay in the driver's seat and never return to the passenger seat.

Top Tips

Whether you use an online planner or a paper diary, spend a little time each day planning how the hours will unfold. A week-to-a-page diary is a perfect at-a-glance representation of where you're investing your energy and helps you ensure you're moving toward the purpose, vision, values, and hopes you most want.

- Take the time to plan your year, your month, and your week.

- Map your habits around the behaviors you most want to develop.

- Keep a daily diary and savor the joy of ticking things off.

- Ask yourself if you are committed to being you.

- Make sure you have a dream team of people urging you on.

- Ensure you're taking responsibility for what you can do.

- Don't allow your fears to hold you back.

- Have your obstacle plan ready and don't use excuses as a way to avoid showing up.

Remember: first we make our habits, and then our habits make us.

Structure is the cornerstone of calmness, clarity, and control.

Part 5

Thrive

Opportunities multiply
as they are seized.

Sun Tzu, Chinese military leader

151

Keep Your Perspective

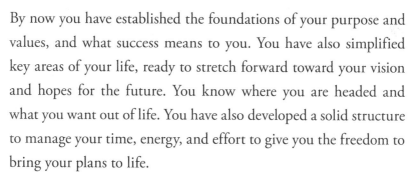

By now you have established the foundations of your purpose and values, and what success means to you. You have also simplified key areas of your life, ready to stretch forward toward your vision and hopes for the future. You know where you are headed and what you want out of life. You have also developed a solid structure to manage your time, energy, and effort to give you the freedom to bring your plans to life.

Of course, now that you have all this figured out, everything will run smoothly. Well, not necessarily. For some of us, there is a real risk in taking these first steps too seriously, a tendency toward perfectionism and becoming workaholics, driving ourselves into the ground. When we lose perspective and our plans start to run us, rather than the other way around, the life we want is always just out of reach.

To navigate our way through the natural lows and highs of life, we need tools to thrive, to buoy our success, and to maintain our energy; the right amount of stress and affirmations to keep us on track; a healthy dose of confidence; and plenty of reasons to laugh. We also need opportunities to stretch ourselves forward with passion projects, travel plans, and bucket lists. We need our own "recipes for success" to guide us toward the lives we most want to live.

Build Your Own Success Toolkit

As you begin to make your purpose, vision, and hopes a reality by consistently following through on your plans, you'll find that even though you show up committed, confident, and courageous, things won't always pan out the way you want.

To maintain your energy and enthusiasm, regardless of how your day is unfolding, create your own success toolkit to help you keep going. Think of this as your equipment for looking after yourself as your journey unfolds.

There are lots of different ways to relax and nurture yourself, so you need to identify the things that work for you. Think beyond soaking in a scented bath or booking a facial—your mind needs to be supported just as much as your body. Working out what keeps you functioning at your best is called self-care, and it's a vital part of your success toolkit.

Cheryl Richardson, author of *The Art of Extreme Self-Care*, sums it up perfectly: "Extreme self-care involves surrounding myself with people who are smart, self-aware, and only interested in two-way relationships. It means taking bold steps, such as eliminating clutter from my life, for good; creating a soul-nourishing work and home environment, and keeping it that way; getting my financial act together so that I always have choices about how to live my life; and not making any commitments whatsoever out of guilt and obligation."

Some Ideas for Your Toolkit

Things you may want to include are:

Authenticity gut check: Are you being *you*? Are you walking the talk and living your values?

Gratitude moments: Are you expressing gratitude for your supporters?

Self-love makeover: Are you looking in the mirror daily and connecting with who you are? Try smiling at your own reflection.

Story audit: Are the stories you're telling yourself creating beliefs that pull you forward?

Sleep bank: Are you decompressing and refueling at night? Remember, sleep is our best medicine.

Acts of kindness: Are you giving to others by performing kind acts? This can be one of the best ways to lower stress levels.

What's working well? Are you building on your strengths to get the results you want?

Jolts of joy: Have you genuinely laughed today?

Grit goal: Are you persisting with things that are a little challenging and celebrating your efforts?

There is no right or wrong answer by which you define success.

Be on Your Own To-Do List

What are you doing for *you* today? This is where you start making sure you're included on your own to-do list. To sustain your optimal level of well-being, you need to take responsibility for scheduling in self-care and treat it as the most important job in the world. This does not mean booking a holiday or shopping trip, but rather a deep level of care. It is about honoring yourself and not succumbing to anxiety or guilt about looking after yourself.

Making pleasure a priority is critical for extreme self-care. Real pleasure is achieved by developing habits that make you feel happy and nurtured. These could include listening to the music you love on your commute to work, drinking your favorite tea each morning, buying flowers for your work desk, going out for dinner every couple of weeks with friends, seeing a movie every month, taking a break from work in the middle of the day to get out into nature, booking a regular pedicure, visiting art galleries, organizing regular walks with friends, or curling up with a book on Sunday afternoons.

Your success toolkit is your immediate go-to when you are feeling a bit out of control, stressed, and stuck. It is your personal backup for when life throws a curveball or you're just worn out and will help put you back in the driver's seat again.

Maintain Your Energy

It's completely within your power to manage your energy levels so they work for you. The human body has basic needs for energy production and maintenance, and addressing them will help you function at your peak. Habits are the key, so ensure your energy toolkit becomes part of your weekly and daily habits, just like brushing your teeth.

Energy Toolkit

Sleep: It is both recovery and preparation. Make sure you're getting at least seven hours a night. If you're having trouble getting to sleep, avoid looking at laptops, smartphones, and tablets for at least an hour before bed. Also, keep your bedroom for sleeping only (no screens allowed!).

Water: Hydrate throughout the day.

Eating habits: Seventy percent of the way you feel is due to what you are eating.

Stretch: Extend your muscles each day.

Move: Get the blood flowing. Many people are starting to use standing desks, as sitting too much is now understood to be dangerous to our health. Standing and moving around regularly also helps you feel more alert.

Mini-pauses: Take five-minute breaks throughout the day.

Attitude: Having a positive attitude gives you energy, while being negative drains you.

Silence: Embrace the stillness surrounding you.

Try a Two-Minute Meditation

A growing body of research suggests we would all benefit from daily meditation. So, how do we integrate it into our lives in a way that's achievable and still gives us the benefits we need?

I meditate in the morning and the evening and have a collection of guided meditations that suit a range of needs for my mind and body. Outside this regular practice, I often sit in silence in the car for a few minutes before the school pickup or when I'm in a line or a traffic jam. It's a small change, but it has had one of the biggest impacts on my physical health and my mindset.

Not sure you can pull it off? Try just two minutes a day. This is much easier and more sustainable than thinking you have to commit to a daily half-hour practice, and you are much more likely to keep at it. You don't need to rush out and buy a meditation cushion, join a class, or even try to sit still for fifteen minutes—not yet. Just start by being still for two minutes each day and noticing your breath. Breathe in and out through your nose, counting slowly to four for the intake and then four for the release. Controlled, calm breathing like this helps us relax, focus, and let go of any stress we may be feeling. It also helps connect our minds to our bodies, which puts us back in the moment and is a powerful tool for mindfulness.

Manage Your Stress

Do you ever feel stressed out? The good news is that a little bit of stress is good for us. It's the body's way of focusing our attention and energy on a particular problem or opportunity, and harnessing all our resources to solve it or move us forward.

But when stress accumulates, hour after hour, day after day, week after week, it starts to wreak havoc on our bodies, our minds, and our relationships. We simply aren't built to handle large amounts of the hormones, such as cortisol and adrenaline, that stress generates. When stress overwhelms us or lingers for too long, it can leave us unable to make decisions, harm our ability to learn, damage our health, and cause us to pull away from others.

Sixty-Second Stress Busters

Here are some fast, tried, and tested ways to reset your stress levels. Spend the time:

- Breathing deeply and slowly

- Stretching

- Drawing a picture

- Sipping a glass of water

- Walking

- Smelling some essential oils

- Standing up and just moving your body

- Answering for yourself, "What is going right?"

- Counting with your eyes closed

- Thinking about the bigger picture to gain perspective

- Laughing

- Putting on a mood-boosting song and singing

- Changing your desktop screen saver to something calming and green

- Answering for yourself, "Will this matter five years from now?"

Reset Yourself

Feeling stressed? I have a list of things I run through to help me refocus and regain a sense of calm. Try it yourself:

I learned today . . .

_____

_____

I'm grateful for . . .

_____

_____

I can let go of . . .

_____

_____

I acknowledge myself today for . . .

_____

_____

I can release the need to be . . .

_____

_____

I choose to enjoy today because . . .

_____

_____

I want to focus on . . .

_____

_____

I believe in myself because . . .

_____

_____

Create Your Affirmations

Your mindset has everything to do with success. Your personal beliefs determine the way you feel and act and ultimately dictate where you'll put your energy. They shape your vision and hopes and affirm what you think is possible when it comes to the kind of success you want to enjoy. If you say you can, you might pull it off. If you say you can't, you'll never get started.

The word *affirmation* comes from the Latin *affirmare*, meaning "to make steady, strengthen." When we put into words what we want to be or what we want to happen, we are empowering ourselves and reassuring our minds about the possibilities.

Affirmations help break the patterns of negative thoughts and move us toward more positive feelings and actions.

Here are some affirmations to get you started:

1. I am happy, healthy, and radiant.

2. I am calm and confident.

3. I am focused and motivated.

4. I choose total well-being.

5. I trust myself.

6. I am light and vibrant.

7. I am proud of who I am.

8. I am exactly where I need to be right now.

9. I am brave. I am bold. I am fierce.

10. I am living my dreams.

11. I am unique.

12. I make a difference.

13. I am open to receiving.

14. I am constantly learning and growing.

15. I am grateful to be alive today.

16. I give myself permission to rest.

17. I protect myself with boundaries.

18. I will achieve greatness.

19. I am beautiful.

20. I choose to feel joy.

Affirmations for wealth:

1. I love money because money loves me.

2. I always have enough money.

3. I am open and willing to receive.

4. Money comes in both expected and unexpected ways.

5. I share my wealth.

6. I embrace the richness of life, in all its forms.

7. I am rewarded for doing what I love.

8. I am open to receiving new sources of income.

9. I trust that life supports and nourishes me.

10. Money comes in unexpected ways.

11. I am abundant.

12. My life is rich in every way.

13. I am worthy, and deserving of wealth.

14. I am a money magnet.

15. I am grateful for money.

16. I am committed.

17. I boldly conquer my money goals.

18. I choose to be wealthy.

19. I am aligned with my purpose.

20. The universe always provides.

Build Your Confidence

How confident do you feel about your ability to create the life you want to be living? Researchers have found that believing we can improve our abilities is actually more important than believing in our abilities themselves. Confidence comes from believing that with the courage to learn, the willingness to make an effort, and the persistence to keep practicing, we're each born with the capacity to make continuous improvements in our lives.

When we have confidence in our ability to grow, we fear failure less, we're not as attached to outcomes, and negative feedback doesn't undo us. Think of Thomas Edison, who persisted through a thousand failed attempts at inventing the lightbulb before he succeeded; now that's confidence! You can build your confidence by:

Using your strengths regularly: These are the things you do well and enjoy. Visit the VIA Institute on Character's website (www.viacharacter.org) for a great tool to help you identify your strengths.

Surrounding yourself with people who love learning: People who are on their own path of growth will be happy to share the journey.

Celebrating efforts, not just results: Don't focus solely on outcomes; acknowledge the efforts you're making along the way.

Sharing your growth: Tell your dream team the small wins and the big results.

Focusing on what's within your control: Know you've made your best effort and let the rest go.

As an achievement junkie with a tendency toward perfectionism, I've found that one of the most effective (and totally unexpected) ways to boost my confidence is to embrace my vulnerability. This means accepting who I am and leaving behind who I think I should be. It allows me to be imperfect and to be okay with this part of my journey, and it significantly increases the depth of my happiness, contentment, and confidence. I might not be the best speaker, have the best book, or cook the best meal for my family, but I'm here, I'm showing up, I'm willing to learn, and I'm willing to accept that makes me good enough.

Author, researcher, and scholar Brené Brown has spent a decade studying vulnerability, courage, worthiness, and shame. She suggests vulnerability is the birthplace of innovation, creativity, and change and that it is our most accurate measurement of courage. It is the gateway to intimacy with ourselves and others. It is about having the confidence to be honest about our fears and how we're feeling and what we need and to be willing to share this with others.

Setting boundaries is a great example. It's something that people don't think about as requiring vulnerability, but saying a gracious no and protecting our time—whether it's family time, creative time, or self-care time—is a huge act of confidence in a culture that values productivity so highly.

Self-confidence is a superpower. Once you start to believe in yourself, magic starts happening.

Remember that confidence is not:

- Trying to be someone else or someone you're not

- Being arrogant or rude

- Fearing being wrong

- Judging others

- Thinking you are the smartest person in the room

- Having an overinflated opinion of yourself

Real confidence starts with you. A confident person uses positive words to build themselves and others up, doesn't need to put others down, knows what their strengths are, understands the importance of self-care, takes responsibility rather than blames, listens more than they talk, is happy to learn from others, and has clear goals and takes action to achieve them.

No one is born with self-confidence. Self-confidence is learned and earned with experience.

Denis Waitley, American writer and speaker

Find Your Joy

When did you last have a really good laugh? You know, one of those outbursts that literally shakes your whole body. When you can hardly breathe and your sides are hurting afterward. If you can't remember the last time you really laughed, it's a clear sign you need to make room for a little more humor and playfulness in your life. Humor balances the seriousness of life, and it's what helps you endure challenges.

While it's great to celebrate achievements and accomplishments, it's just as important to enjoy the journey—and this is where laughter plays a huge role. It may not be a cure-all, but laughter is good for you on many levels.

Laughter relaxes your whole body: A good, hearty laugh relieves physical tension and stress, relaxing your muscles for up to forty-five minutes afterward.

Laughter triggers the release of endorphins: The body's natural feel-good chemicals, endorphins, promote an overall sense of well-being.

Laughter boosts the immune system: It decreases stress hormones and increases your body's production of white blood cells and infection-fighting antibodies, thus improving your resistance to disease.

Laughter protects the heart: Laughter improves the function of blood vessels and increases blood flow, which can help protect against heart attack and other cardiovascular problems.

Ways to Laugh More

You can find more reasons to laugh by:

Smiling: This is where laughter begins, so find reasons to smile and let it take over your body.

Spending time with fun, playful people: Seek out family and friends who make you laugh.

Moving toward laughter: When you hear people laughing, join them; laughter is highly contagious.

Joining a laughter club: These are groups that get together for the express purpose of laughing.

Watching comedy: This can be in any form you like—a YouTube clip, live act, television show, or movie.

Reading funny books or comics: Start each day with a funny quote or cartoon.

What or who makes you laugh? Invest some recovery time in these activities and people.

The most important friendship you can have is with yourself.

Embrace
Your Passions

Is there something you do just for the love of it? Not necessarily to make money. Not necessarily for fame and accolades. But just because it indulges your deep desire to create. To bring your ideas to life, in whatever form they may take.

It could be a hobby, such as painting, gardening, or playing an instrument. It could be a community project, such as coaching your kids' sports team, organizing the annual street party, or providing companionship at the local seniors' center.

Passion projects and hobbies are vital for fostering growth and development. They ensure we don't end up regretting the things we wish we'd done, and they offer stress relief, lower stress hormones, stave off burnout, provide pleasure and gratification, and keep life full of color and vitality.

Choose Your Passions

Here are some examples to get you going, remembering that whatever you want to do, it needs to be built into your habit map or journal to ensure you find the time to make it happen.

- Photography

- Gardening

- Reading

- Writing

- Cooking

- Movies

- Golf

- Swimming

- Playing an instrument

- Singing

- Sports

- Yoga

- Drawing and painting

- Dancing

- Knitting

What is your passion project? What can you see yourself doing for a long time so that you become passionate about it?

Travel
with Intention

Where do you long to visit? What amazing things would you like to do when you get there? Whenever you travel with purpose, more world abundance opens up to you, more relationships are created, and most importantly, you can incorporate some of your bucket list and hobbies into your trip.

Holidays can be incredible experiences when you travel to learn, meet new people, and grow as a person. Trips with an intention, such as photography tours, art adventures, cooking classes, and golf holidays, can be particularly rewarding, as can trips where you are giving back, such as going overseas to do volunteer work.

These are some of the memories you savor in life because you come home feeling inspired.

Get online and start a detailed investigation of the places you would like to visit. Look beyond the main tourist sites to find opportunities to get off the beaten path and put yourself in areas where you'll be more likely to meet the locals and experience their way of life. It's hard to truly understand a different culture when you're viewing it through the windows of a car or bus. Here are some questions to ask yourself when you're researching your next trip:

- What is my intention for this adventure?

- What could I learn as I go?

- How could I immerse myself in this culture?

- What opportunities does this offer me?

- What would make this trip memorable?

Step Out of Your Comfort Zone

If your life is starting to feel a little dull and boring, it's a sure sign your comfort zone needs stretching. When we take on new opportunities or challenges, there's a natural learning curve that comes with mastering new ways of thinking, feeling, and being. Over time, we get better at putting the pieces together to get the results we want, adapting to this new way of life and settling into a comfortable groove. This feeling of comfort is a place of peace and relief, but if we remain comfortable and unchallenged for too long, we stagnate and become bored.

For me, traveling overseas on my own, taking on jobs I thought were too hard, and continually looking for ways to stretch myself have led to personal growth, increased life satisfaction, and happiness. Things can go wrong, but having resilience, perspective, and a good foundation of values to fall back on makes this process exciting.

Your comfort zone is a place where you are familiar; essentially it is your routine. There is very little stress in the comfort zone, and that is where you feel most relaxed and safe. A routine sets you up with a foundational support structure, and life becomes very easy. With a routine, you can have some rest, be a bit productive, and take a break. Staying in your comfort zone for extended periods of time is like having a vacation in only one place with the same food and the same people. As pleasurable as it feels in routine, it can quickly start to lose its vibrance. Treat your comfort zone like a home base and venture into the world to grow and evolve.

Stepping out of your comfort zone from time to time can lead to great personal achievement and growth. Who doesn't want that? The reason is simple—if you stay inside your comfort zone all the time, nothing changes. You don't grow. You're not challenged. You don't get to find out what you're made of. Instead, you're comfortable. Life's easy. The unique recipe for your comfort zone is determined by your long list of dreams and desires that you haven't achieved. Chances are if your list is long, then you need to step outside your comfort zone more often and start ticking things off your list.

Most successful people are in the constant habit of stepping out in both big things and small, continually exercising the habit, and reinforcing their confidence to live a greater life. Your dreams won't come to you; you have to step out of your comfort zone and chase them down. Stepping out of your comfort zone is something you can learn step-by-step. The more you practice, the easier it will be. Set yourself small, manageable goals, like taking a different walking path to work, taking up salsa dancing, or going out and ordering something new, and reap the benefits it has to offer.

We all live within comfort zones in different areas of our lives. What does your comfort zone look like? Are you:

- Holding back from starting a new business?

- Staying in a relationship that is okay, when in your heart you know you want out?

- Putting food in your body that you know doesn't improve your health?

- Staying in your job and not pushing for a challenging promotion?

- Surrounding yourself with a cluttered environment?

- Surrounding yourself with people who don't hold you to your highest potential?

Too often we let our mistakes and setbacks define us. But it's really our attitude toward failure that determines whether it's going to be an experience from which we can learn and grow or one that stops us in our tracks. Each year, I set a monthly challenge that's a little out of my comfort zone so that I can foster my continual growth.

Test Your Comfort Zone

Commit: Get out of your comfort zone as often as possible. If you don't challenge yourself and make yourself a little uncomfortable, you won't grow, evolve, and flourish as a human being.

Keep learning: Make sure you're always a little bit "green," as it means you're still trying new things and have the capacity to learn. And realize that there's always room for improvement.

Crawl, walk, run: Don't force yourself to leap into the deep end immediately. Break down bigger goals into smaller chunks, and slowly take on more daring challenges.

Be curious: Throw away your assumptions about what will happen and get curious instead.

Mix it up: Experiment with activities you wouldn't normally do. Numbers geek? Try a course in meditation. IT guru? Enroll in cooking classes. Creative thinker? Sign up for martial arts. Open up new sides of yourself and explore them!

Invite the adventure of the new day ahead
and look forward to the experiences it brings.

Create Your
Bucket List

What do you want to do before you die? Put simply, a bucket list is a list of things you really want to do before you die—a play on the phrase *kick the bucket*.

What do your boldest dreams entail? These might be big dreams, such as traveling the world. They might be smaller ambitions, such as playing the guitar publicly. Whatever the size, you have to work toward them just as you work toward your goals, which is why it's important to write them down. By creating a bucket list, you turn your dreams into attainable, tangible goals that are within your reach.

Your bucket list is there to inspire, to represent your values, to put fire in your belly, and to excite your brain. Whenever I read something that inspires and appeals to me, I write it on my bucket list so I always feel that I am moving forward. One of the ways I like to do this is by creating a twenty-year plan. It sounds daunting, but it is the simplest thing to do as it creates perspective instantly.

Think about it for a moment. Where will you be in twenty years? When an age is attached to the question, a vague picture of what your life might be like emerges; it also gives ages to the people around you—your partner, your children, your parents, and your friends. Suddenly, you can see what stage of life you'll be at in twenty years, and that helps you start to picture what you want your life to look like at that point.

Your Bucket List

Think about the following areas and what you'd like to achieve in each:

Career	Adventure
Recreation	Fitness
Knowledge	Spiritual
Activities	Investments
Travel	Education
Family	Personal growth
Home	Fun
Friends	Service

Boldly Embrace Your Twenty-Year Plan

Start with a blank piece of paper or spreadsheet.

Create four columns: Year, Career, Home, and Family.

Write in things you're sure of: your age in twenty years, plus your partner's and kids' ages, your stage of life, your health, and your career. Once this solid, knowable information is plugged in, it makes it easier to open your mind up to dream big.

List every holiday you dream of taking and every hobby you want to develop. Look at your twenty-year plan and work out where your milestone birthdays and anniversaries will fall. Start thinking about the celebrations you'd like to create and dates when you may be able to match up your dream holiday destinations with major milestones.

Add other things from your bucket list and when you'd like to make them happen.

Think about education—are there courses or further study you or your partner would like to undertake? If you have children, think about where you would like them to attend school, both primary and secondary.

Consider your living arrangements too. Are you already in your dream home or would you like to renovate or move house? Are you happy with where you live or do you hope to move to another area further down the track? Will you need to upsize or downsize at some point? When would you like to retire?

What Is Your Recipe for Success?

Everyone has their own definition of success, and these can vary considerably. Rather than relying on a one-size-fits-all definition, it's important to devise your own recipe for success to guide you through life. It needs to be something you'll see often, so that it becomes a part of who you are and can influence your decisions on a daily basis. I recommend programming it into your weekly plan. When I ask my clients to create their recipe for success, I suggest they use the word *success* as an acronym:

S: Sort out your values.

U: Understand your beliefs and behaviors.

C: Choose your vision for yourself.

C: Construct hopes to support your vision and brand.

E: Evaluate and acknowledge each step of your journey and progress.

S: Simplify and structure your processes.

S: Smile and enjoy your ideal setup for optimal living and success.

Success means freedom of choice in my daily life.

Success means living a purposeful life.

Recap

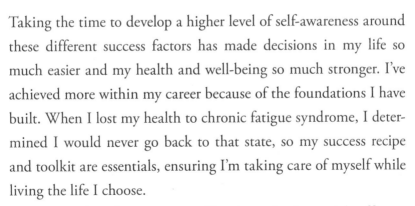

Taking the time to develop a higher level of self-awareness around these different success factors has made decisions in my life so much easier and my health and well-being so much stronger. I've achieved more within my career because of the foundations I have built. When I lost my health to chronic fatigue syndrome, I determined I would never go back to that state, so my success recipe and toolkit are essentials, ensuring I'm taking care of myself while living the life I choose.

As your plans begin to pay off and you begin to tick off your successes, you need to have the tools to maintain the life you're creating. Drawing on your success toolkit, maintaining your energy, and ensuring you have the right amount of stress, plenty of reasons to laugh, affirmations to move you forward, and enough confidence to keep pulling it all off will help you navigate the inevitable highs and lows we all experience. Along the way, keep stretching beyond your comfort zone by making time for your passion projects, creating your twenty-year bucket list, and staying true to your own recipe for success.

Top Tips

- Embed your energy toolkit into your weekly habits and daily actions—make time for self-care.

- Collect and store the affirmations that work for you.

- Start a gratitude jar, journal, or photo book.

- Try to meditate for two minutes each day.

- In the shower, check on your breathing. Before you go to sleep, make sure you are breathing correctly.

- Make your passwords something you want to be or are aiming for so that you are typing a daily affirmation when you enter them.

- Start a bucket list book, or twenty-year plan.

- Write on your bathroom mirror whatever you need in order to maintain confidence for the day or week.

- Practice being vulnerable with others about how you're feeling and asking for what you need.

- Book stress busters. My phone is constantly reminding me to breathe.

- Schedule time for your hobbies.

- Have the courage to be uncomfortable when you are trying new things.

- Book a trip with purpose and intention.

- Prepare food for tomorrow and fill your water bottle each weeknight.

- Create your to-do list for the next day the night before.

- Make a rule of no phones when eating.

Plant the seeds for success and nurture them, and you will be rewarded with a life that blooms.

Part 6

Refuel

Taking a pause is exciting,
invigorating, life changing,
and possible. Taking time out
to see life from a different
perspective, or country, can
give you the energy
and creativity to live
life optimally.

Take Time Off

Taking a pause in life was something I had heard of but didn't think was possible. You can only do it when you are young and responsibility-free, right? When I was twenty-one years old, I traveled the world with a backpack for two years, and I think that was probably the time I learned the most in life—a sense of freedom that came hand in hand with fear, excitement, opportunity, fun, loneliness, self-acceptance, and incredible experiences, both good and bad, which I have always treasured.

New York graphic designer and TED speaker Stefan Sagmeister takes a year off every seven years, saying he will retire five years later in his life to balance it all out. Listen to his talk titled "The

Power of Time Off," and you will see that, with the right planning, a sabbatical can be one of the smartest career moves you can make. Why wait until retirement? Why not have these incredible experiences along the way to gain clarity and energy? Taking these breaks when we are fit enough to challenge ourselves, do what we want, and experience the world in new ways really makes sense.

Before you say a sabbatical is not for you, let's debunk a few myths.

Myth	Reality
I cannot afford it professionally.	You really won't miss much while you're away.
It's unaffordable financially.	It is approximately half a year's salary—spread over a lifetime, it's not that much.
We can't take the kids out of school.	I would argue that our children learned more on our trip—science, geography, physical education, biology, English, cultural studies, history, anthropology, mechanics, engineering, art, photography, psychology, humanities, popular culture, community life, economics, life skills, orienteering, positive role-modeling, you name it!

If I can't afford to travel overseas, is there any point?	There are plenty of amazing experiences to be had on our own doorstep. You might like to visit the woods; explore a state you haven't visited before; do a house swap in another city; stay on a working farm and experience shearing and mustering; go camping; live on an island; rent a beach house; explore the rainforest; or take part in an environmental and wildlife conservation project.
I need to wait until retirement.	Life is unpredictable—you don't know what your health will be like or how long you'll live.
Successful people don't have time for sabbaticals.	Successful people take sabbaticals to gain clarity, energy, and motivation.
It is impossible to plan.	You'll make it happen if you want to; just book it, and everything else will fall into place.
It is just a holiday and won't change my work/life in any way.	It is a major life experience; you'll learn, evolve, grow, and develop your human self. It is a chance to reboot!
When I get back, my career will be on the rocks.	You'll be able to offer more to your career if you are not resentful of it.

Map Out a Plan

When our children were born, my husband and I went through our twenty-year plan, basically covering when our children would start school, when they would start secondary school, and when they would finish. We asked ourselves a few simple questions: When would we like to take a pause in life? When would it be possible? What ages would work best for us? What would be the optimal time for our children to travel and experience the world with us? What would we regret not doing? How could we make it happen?

We penciled in two years where we thought it would be possible, when our kids wouldn't need to do homework and could just be kids. We also had other criteria—our son and daughter had to be old enough to bike, walk, and experience the world. We named our sabbatical The Pause, and we called all the steps required to get there "Operation Too Easy." I have to say that it is the best thing I have done in my life: a beautiful, incredibly special, and inspiring trip that I will treasure forever. Of course, I am already planning the next one.

A Sabbatical
or a Career Break?

What is the difference between the two? Well, a sabbatical is when you take your time out and return to your job with the blessing of your employer. It is a time where many employers assist employees to take a business course, do volunteer work, or travel. (I know of an enlightened company that supported a senior employee to do yoga teacher training.) The idea is always to return to the company and continue with the organization that has supported the sabbatical.

A career break is when you resign and consciously take a break. Many people do this before setting up their own business. They take time to breathe, plan, learn languages, write that script they've always wanted to, spend some time at home with their family, or simply take stock of life. Many people take one before changing their career path.

Questions to Help You Gain Clarity

- Do you want a break?

- Do you need time to rest, recharge, recommit?

- What would make your working life shine?

- What do you want to learn?

- How much will it cost?

- Will your current employer be open to it?

- Will your business suffer?

- What will it do for your health?

- Where do you dream of going?

- Who else has done this, and what was their experience?

The only way to take a break in life, or press the pause button,
is to make the decision that you want to take it.

Plan a Break

Taking a break is part of your plan if you want it to be. Remember that you know your values, your vision, your goals, your structures, and your passion projects or hobbies. And in the same way that our cars need refueling, our technical tools need recharging, and our soil needs fertilizing, our minds need space to be able to think and our bodies need to move, stretch, and breathe to be able to function optimally.

To press the pause button, the first step is to make the decision that you want to do this. Make the decision and tell someone. When my husband and I decided, we wrote it down in our planner and looked at it. It looked great, but then our emotions ran crazy. Can we really do that? What would people think? What would happen to our jobs? How could we afford it? Wow, how bold would we be if we did that? This turned quite quickly into: We can do it! Wouldn't it be great; how adventurous and how glorious would it be to have freedom and a blank slate each day? Imagine seeing the world through the eyes of our children; imagine leaving the phones behind.

EXAMPLE
Mara's Break from Work

Mara chose to take a break after taking on a new executive role in the nonprofit sector. She chose a six-week window where she asked her husband and friends around her not to discuss her professional life. She began an online drawing class and spent time decorating her new home office. She planned a range of catch-up lunches with friends she normally doesn't have time to see and also added a weekend caring for her granddaughter so that her daughter could enjoy a bit of a break too. Time for podcasts, organizing financial affairs, and a couple of weeks at her favorite beach made the break life-affirming, allowing her to start her new role completely rested and focused.

Diane's Break from Alcohol and Social Media

Diane created a new sense of spaciousness by deciding not to drink alcohol or go on social media for twelve months as she settled into her new home in a coastal community. While she was concerned she would miss out on what was happening by not being on Instagram, she quickly discovered that her levels of anxiety dropped, she was comparing herself to others less, and she was not thinking about what to post next. By not drinking, her skin began to glow, she found she still enjoyed socializing with all the new non-alcoholic drinks available, and she loved all the money she was saving by not buying bottles of wine.

A pause can provide gifts and abundance that money can't buy.

I left my phone in Melbourne and got on the plane.
I did not make a phone call for twenty weeks. And I lived!

Design Your Pause

Here is how you can start planning:

- Why do you want a pause?

- How much time do you want? What would the start and end date be?

- Do you want land, sea, mountains, oceans, lakes?

- What will be different from where you are now?

- What is on your bucket list or in your dreams that you can incorporate?

- How would you finance your sabbatical?

- How would you structure your time?

- How would you re-enter the workforce?

- What is the purpose? What do you want to learn from this valuable time?

Our Big Pause Story—Five Months

Where: United States, British Virgin Islands, Mexico

When: 2013

Who: My husband and me, our two children, and an aunt and grandparent for part of the time

How long: Twenty weeks

Essentials: A great attitude, courage, fear, a plan, and my camera

Contraband items: Smartphones, watches, makeup, clients, high heels, suits, and fancy clothes

Goal: To explore, to connect, to bond, to experience, to learn, to secure meaning, and to recharge body and mind

The outcome: Freedom, energy, fun, adventures of a lifetime, new skills, stories, and a feeling of great abundance in life. A sense that we are in charge of our own destiny, so keep planning for greatness and depth in life. Oh, and we all liked each other!

When we decided to take our pause, it was important that we had clarity on the purpose. I wanted to recharge my body and mind. I wanted to have the time to learn photography and capture the moments that would help me be mindful and present and enjoy the moment. My husband, Michael, had been a CEO for ten years and was really in need of a break and recharge. Our ten years of marriage had been incredible so far, with two booming careers, the births of two children who were now in school, marathons run, house renovated, and a full commitment to being who we wanted to be. It was time to take a breath, to enjoy, to savor, to celebrate, to stop.

Our Plan

Altitude living: Eight weeks in Colorado, at almost seven thousand feet above sea level in Steamboat Springs. Hiking, biking, fishing, reading, photography, yoga, exercising, breathing, and decompressing from the world.

The Road Bear RV: Six weeks on the road, covering nearly four thousand miles across Utah, Colorado, Nevada, and California, experiencing people, cities, nature, animals, and roadhouses, taking photographs, and renewing our wedding vows in Las Vegas.

A change of season: Back to Colorado for three weeks to see the leaves begin to turn in autumn, visit the rodeos, ride horses, and recalibrate our bodies and minds, do yoga, read, and see the first snowfall of the season.

A Caribbean calypso: Two weeks in the British Virgin Islands in the Caribbean. Charter and drive our own boat. Swim, snorkel, live on the boat, meet people, and experience ocean, sand, navigation, photography, fishing, heat, and the Caribbean way of life.

Signing off from Cancun: One week in Cancun, Mexico. Rest and prepare to re-enter our lives of career, work, school, family, activities, learning, sports, and so on.

A pause is taking time to breathe, to enjoy,
to savor, to celebrate, to stop.

A Peek in Our Writing Journals

Before you begin your sabbatical, or pause, it is a great time to journal, as it's a useful way to explore your thoughts, fears, and expectations about the changes ahead.

Shannah

There are so many emotions now that I have stopped working. I am an achievement junkie, so it is exciting to have the opportunity to think about achievement in new ways. I am excited to experience new things and, being a beach person, to see what it is like to be a mountain person. I am excited to have time: time to explore, feel, learn, grow, be in the moment, and master more of myself, work on being the best version of me I can be in life. And I'm excited to get out of Melbourne in winter; I really struggle with the cold.

I'm also feeling fear about leaving my beloved routines and structures and anxiety that I may not actually like being in a pause. That sounds quite bizarre, but I love my job, my home, my existence here in Melbourne. The what-ifs are there in my mind. What if I don't like it? What if I don't get the space I need as a person who likes calm in her life? What if I don't like being with the kids round the clock? I have to challenge myself to have no expectations of the family or the places, and to enjoy everything for what it is.

I am filled with determination to learn. To learn more about photography, about life, about computers and IT, as I am falling behind. Michael is our IT department, and I have let him be that, but I need to learn how it all works, so I can help myself. I want to think about the next stage of our lives and what I need to do to capture and enjoy every moment.

I am feeling gratitude, bucketloads of it. Firstly, that we are fortunate enough to be able to do this trip. I am grateful that Michael and I are both adventurous and courageous enough to make the bold decisions and make things happen for ourselves. Neither of us wait for opportunities; we both go out and make them. I am grateful I have the courage to leave my business for a while and let it breathe, to be authentic and live the life I have chosen. I have incredible gratitude for my marriage, and that we operate as a team, that we have had the best ten years, and that each year seems to get better, faster, and more exciting than the last.

But mostly, I am deeply happy. With my life, with my marriage, with my beautiful children. We are all healthy, physically and mentally. And this is why I want to take a pause—to deeply experience this.

Michael

Well, here I am. Sitting in Dubai, after a work trip, about to jump on a plane and spend fourteen hours flying home before packing up and heading off on another thirty-hour journey in six days' time. Normally, this would be something to dread; however, this time I can't wait to jump into row fifty-nine with my family and begin a trip we'll remember for the rest of our lives.

I've always had a strong motivation to take time out and spend five months overseas as a family unit. Firstly, because of my vivid, fond childhood memories of an extended road trip with my family, and secondly, because I believe we owe it to ourselves to stop, think, and work out how the hell we got to where we are today and how we can continue to make our lives awesome in the future.

I am proud we take risks. I am proud we act, rather than talk, and I am most proud that we have done it all by ourselves with no help from anyone. There is little doubt life will throw curveballs at us from time to time, but this trip will be a bonding experience that will be ours and ours alone.

I think the reason I have managed to be successful in my job and my life over the past ten years is mostly due to Shannah—how amazing she is at home, in business, and in life. She sets standards that don't allow me to drop my guard or accept the easy path. It has become second nature for me to take chances and follow my instincts.

I love my kids. I love spending quality time with them. I hope to find a new level of connection and calm in our relationship.

I look forward to bonding with them both. We are a close family, but there is more work to do there.

I can't wait to go home to the mountains. In some funny way, I know they have been a big part of my life. I love the casualness and informality—mountain people don't take themselves too seriously, but they really appreciate and love the environment around them.

I'm looking forward to learning new skills. It has been a long time since I actually started something from scratch, as a beginner. Whether it is biking, fishing, or RV-ing, I am looking forward to learning again.

So, let's embrace the pause, open our minds, get on that plane, and get the hell out of Hampton for a while! Bring it on.

Reading these predeparture journals again after our trip really heightened what we got out of it. We had a greater appreciation for the bold steps we had taken to make sure that what we wanted most in life actually happened, and I realized that my fears about being away for so long were unfounded.

Writing journals before and after holidays or before a big deal is made, or even just writing down thoughts and emotions, can be really helpful in aiding our growth and evolution. The more we understand ourselves and take ownership of our lives, the richer they will be.

Summary

Only you can dictate the path of your life and orchestrate what you want to happen. You have to make those decisions and have the courage to take an informed risk to make your dreams come true.

Our pause strengthened our marriage and our bonds as a family and gave us gifts that went beyond the financial cost—experiences I will treasure for the rest of my life. It did cost money, but we saved, budgeted, and took the risk, and it delivered.

216

Recap

- Five months is not a long time.

- You need to have a basic plan, but make sure you leave space for spontaneity.

- Your attitude needs to be in the right place.

- You don't need much in life.

- If you want to live your dream, you need to book it and make it happen.

- You need an intention for your time out.

- Taking a break from your busy life is an exceptional way to connect and strengthen family bonds.

- Experiences are educational; your children will learn important life skills.

- Disconnecting is a great way to recharge.

- It's your break, so do your research and make sure it ticks as many of your boxes as possible (rather than the well-meaning suggestions of others!).

- Be realistic. Plan a break that is achievable and that you know you can budget for.

Remember, no matter how long you take,
nothing significant will have changed when you get back;
only you will have grown, evolved, and experienced.

Top Tips

- Do you want mini-breaks in your life, or do you want to wait until retirement to have one big break?

- Plan with intention.

- Tell people your plans; this may open doors through friends of friends wherever you're going and it will also help firm up your commitment.

- You may like to consider a house swap.

- Write down where you want to go and what you want to achieve.

- Draw up a timeline of your life and plot where you want the breaks to be.

- Factor in some downtime, particularly at the end of the break. A mixture of action, adventure, rest, and relaxation is ideal.

- Search the internet for interesting things that happen around the time of your break. Cultural festivals, animal migrations, natural phenomena (such as the northern lights), and landscapes that are particularly beautiful in certain seasons (snowcapped mountains or wildflowers blooming) can all add to a break immeasurably.

- A slow pace gives us time to meet people, absorb a culture, and experience daily life in different surroundings. Not to mention time to rest! Try not to race from one sight to the next.

- Encourage everyone going along on your adventure to keep a journal.

Your time is limited, so don't waste it living someone else's life.

Steve Jobs, American entrepreneur

Part 7

Shine

Find ecstasy in life;
the mere sense of living
is joy enough.

Emily Dickinson, American poet

Claim Your Personal Power

For me, this is the fun part: helping people create the lives they most want to be living. You see, after a while, you might find that while everything is going along nicely, suddenly you want to quit, you feel bored, or you start sabotaging yourself in a whole new way.

Why do we do this to ourselves? We're hardwired with a tremendous capacity to adapt to nearly all the good and bad things that happen in our lives. Whether it's a new relationship, a new job, improved health, or newfound wealth, over time the shine starts to wear off and these hard-won changes in our lives start to deliver fewer and fewer rewards.

Unfortunately, while the thrill of victory and the agony of defeat have been found to abate over time, it appears we adapt much faster to the things we most enjoy. In fact, scientists believe we're prone to eventually take for granted pretty much every good thing that happens to us. It's why our energy, well-being, and happiness often seem like they don't last.

If you feel you're starting to stagnate—physically, mentally, emotionally, or spiritually—despite all the wonderful changes you've been making, it's important to know you're simply adapting and that this is a completely normal part of human functioning. To see how you're doing, quickly check in with these questions:

- How do you feel now?

- How is your confidence tracking?

- Where is your integrity sitting?

- Are your thoughts clear, strong, and energetic?

- Have you fully embraced the fact that you are in the driver's seat?

- Do you rise and shine?

- Are you practicing patience and mindfulness?

- Do your habits serve you well?

- Do your body, mind, and soul feel healthy?

- Are you grateful for what's unfolding?

If you're not consistently flourishing, in this chapter you'll discover how you can prevent, slow down, and even ward off stagnation altogether by paying more attention to what's happening, keeping life varied and dynamic, savoring and appreciating the changes, surprising yourself, making your activities more novel, and staying with your purpose.

Embrace
Mindfulness

Is your life running you, or are you running it? With so much going on all the time, it's easy for life to slip away, despite our best intentions. As I first shared in "Clarify Your Purpose," to help stay on track, I start each day with this question: What is my purpose today?

I find it easiest to answer this question by journaling. It's a private window to my soul that allows me to constantly check in with how things are really going. Journaling is for you and only you. It is the business of you. It is how you personally transform, grow, and adapt as you consciously work on living a life you love. When we write, we gain true clarity on where we are at the moment and where we want to be growing. Where do we need to change and adapt to evolve?

When you write for yourself, you don't need to edit or spell-check; you just let it all flow. You can pour what is in your mind onto paper, and during that process, you learn, question, grow, and take ownership. This process can transform your life. Be honest with yourself, avoid self-criticism and editing, and don't hold yourself back.

Choose whatever form of journal works best for you: a notebook, diary, computer file, or scrapbook; hard or soft cover; lined or unlined; colorful or black-and-white; free-form or structured.

Things to Include

Add words, drawings, pictures, photos, quotes, lists, websites, and more, but most of all, put in here yourself and your own precious thoughts. By writing down your thoughts, ideas, and feelings, you are hardwiring yourself for optimal living.

Initiating Thoughts

If you're new to journaling, fill in the chart here and use it as a guide to get your thoughts flowing.

Feelings
Goals
Dreams
Responsibilities
Achievements
Relationships
Health (Mental and Physical)

Stay Focused

Where attention goes, energy flows. By this stage, you know more about yourself than you did when you started this process. You know how to structure your purpose and values into your days through your carefully designed planner, which takes into account every aspect of your life. But this journey isn't just about organization. The real purpose of harnessing these strategies is so you can stop fretting about getting everything done and instead relax in the knowledge that everything has been allocated its own time and space, allowing you to be fully present and enjoy each moment.

Wherever you are—at home, on a plane, in a meeting—if you are fully present, you can live life with depth, clarity, and a sense of total abundance. Mindfulness brings calm and self-awareness, so you can make well-informed decisions each hour of the day. It can be practiced all day, every day.

I like to use the five senses (sight, hearing, taste, smell, touch) to guide my mindfulness practice. By engaging my senses, I can take control and find calm, even in the most stressful situations. Consider how a particular smell can trigger a happy memory. Perhaps it's the scent of roses taking you back to afternoon tea at your grandmother's house. The smells wafting out of a bakery may remind you of cooking with the kids (and lots of flour explosions, spoon licking, and giggles). It is incredibly powerful to tap into these types of golden moments on a daily basis, simply by being mindful enough to engage your senses.

Connect with Your Five Senses

Sight: Look, acknowledge, see. Notice the view, the formation of clouds, the brilliant colors that are abundant in nature.

Sound: Listen with closed eyes to what is happening around you. Also, listen to silence: it is powerful and re-energizing, and you can hear yourself breathing. When you need to block out distracting sounds, try white noise or the apps playing the sound of rain.

Smell: Your sense of smell can change your hormone levels and promote calm. Soap with essential oils, just-baked bread, freshly ground coffee—all of these scents can alter your state of mind and reduce your stress levels. Likewise, synthetic perfumes can often make you feel ill or stressed out, so avoid these where possible.

Taste: Be present for all your meals and savor every mouthful and how it makes you feel, such as the clean taste of a crisp apple or a hot coffee reaching your belly.

Touch: When you acknowledge the different textures around you—skin, a soft blanket, a sandy beach, and so on—and think about how they make you feel, you can slow down time.

Mindfulness brings calm and a greater level of self-awareness,
helping you make well-informed decisions each hour of the day.

Favorite Sensory Experiences

If we train ourselves to become more aware of the ordinary, life can quickly become extraordinary. Mindful eating, mindful walking, mindful talking, and mindful living make life amazing! Jot down the things you enjoy from a sensory perspective:

Taste *e.g. salted caramels.*

Touch *e.g. patting your pet.*

Sound *e.g. rain on a tin roof.*

Smell *e.g. freshly cut grass.*

Sight *e.g. admiring local architecture.*

Add Some Spice
to Your Life

Feeling a little bored and seeing grayness in every direction of your life? This is a sure sign it's time to spice things up.

Our brains love novelty, so when we have adapted to our well-being practices, even the most tested approaches can stop bringing us much joy. But don't throw the baby out with the bathwater. Instead, think about what you can do to mix things up or do things a little differently, or even just give them a rest for a while and then come back to them a few weeks later.

The tiniest changes make us feel refreshed and renewed; they don't have to be big and too hard—even a new coffee cup can make us feel great! Try some of these approaches to spice things up:

- Create a treasure box of all your favorite golden moments using photos, letters, mementos, and the like.

- Commit to an exercise you've never tried before.

- Make a list of ten new places to visit.

- Read three classic novels.

- Explore a new restaurant each month.

- Reconnect with old friends you haven't seen for ages.

- Take a hike somewhere you've never been before.

- Rearrange your desk, furniture, and cupboards and declutter a little bit more; out with the old, in with the new.

- Set yourself mini-challenges for mindfulness.

- Be a tourist in your own town.

- Check your clothing. Is it tired and old? Does it make you feel confident? Maybe it's time for a new look!

Remember, adaptation is just a normal part of life, so if you're feeling a little bored, it's your brain's way of telling you to mix it up.

EXAMPLE

Jerry's Spice in Life

Jerry is the kind of man who had many successes in his personal life and professional career. His parents pushed him to be the best in everything at a very early age. Because of this, Jerry could never relax and was always worried he would be letting his family down if he didn't work diligently to be successful. Jerry found himself working seven days a week and had no hobbies. I worked together with Jerry to help him identify the things that might bring him joy outside the workplace. He was open to trying different things to add some spice to his life. Jerry discovered photography, which ignited a spark of passion, and he was soon spending his free time walking in nature taking pictures of flowers. Jerry took a chance, and as a result, he also began to appreciate himself for who he is and learned to embrace his artistic self.

EXAMPLE

Andrea's Spice in Life

Andrea is the kind of person who is always giving her time to others. She takes care of her older parents, works full-time, and volunteers at a local animal shelter. Her sense of responsibility to the well-being of others caused her to fall into a rut. She knew this way of living would persist unless she started to make time for herself as well. I worked with Andrea and found her love of animals brought her immense joy. Andrea decided to adopt a rescue dog named Zoe and began teaching her tricks. The happiness and unconditional love Andrea felt from working with Zoe lifted her spirits and provided an outlet for exercise, and soon Andrea was meeting new people at the local dog park. Andrea's next goal is to help Zoe become a therapy dog so she can bring joy to others. Andrea's life is still very full, but she now prioritizes her own happiness and looks forward to the adventures of every day.

Have Fun

People often ask me, "If you are so organized and committed, where's the fun?" The fun is in every day! The fun is in my attitude and not taking myself too seriously. Being organized lets me be spontaneous without sacrificing all the great work I'm doing.

Unfortunately, as we grow up, too many of us stop playing. "Don't be childish." "Stop wasting time." "Quit messing around." Most of us hear these criticisms as we start to move away from childhood, and the result is that by the time we've become adults, we've forgotten the growth and joy that playing brings to our lives. But the truth is, we are built to play and built through play. It is what makes us feel truly alive. Giving yourself permission to embrace a sense of spontaneity and fun can restore a healthy sense of play in the life you're living.

Playtime can involve anything from simply being silly to playing a sport, spending time doing something you love, or catching up with friends and having fun. The aim is to have a laugh, relax, and most importantly, let go and enjoy yourself. It can't be forced, and you won't enjoy it if you're not feeling comfortable, so do whatever works for you (pranks and acting up might be right up one person's alley but leave someone else feeling foolish). It may seem a little strange at first, especially if you haven't allowed play into your life for a long time, but soon you'll be right back in the swing of things.

I find that I need a weekly dose of fun, so I make it happen as often as I can to help me stay connected to the simple joys of life and the magic that comes from playing.

Ways to Start Playing

- Memorize a few good jokes.

- Start a hobby just for the fun of it.

- Have a virtual vacation—"go to Italy" for the day with some friends by eating Italian food, drinking Italian wine, and seeing an Italian movie, for example.

- When running the bath for the kids, jump in yourself.

- Turn the music up and get your groove going.

- Change your look.

- Roll down a hill.

- Gaze at the clouds and find shapes within them.

- Go to a big sporting event and cheer your heart out.

- Listen to a seashell.

- Play golf with your friends.

- Make a photo album of your funniest pictures and photos.

- Go on a zip line and get some thrills.

- Gallop down a hallway as though you are riding a horse.

- Start a regular family games night with your board games and cards.

- See a musical or comedy show.

- Go away for the weekend on a last-minute deal.

- Build the biggest and best sandcastle on the beach.

- Call a friend and go out and have fun.

Savor and Celebrate Your Success

Have you ever been so focused on success that you had no time to celebrate what you were achieving? I know it sounds crazy, but many of us are so busy striving to reach our goals we forget to make time to truly savor and appreciate the incredible outcomes we're creating. Yet people who revel in their successes are far more likely to enjoy them. It also helps to program your brain for more success to come.

Ways You Can Savor and Celebrate Success

- Share it with others.

- Throw a dinner party to celebrate.

- Take a mental picture of the moment and how you're feeling.

- Create a memento to remember what you've achieved.

- Shout for joy.

- Immerse yourself in the feeling of success.

- Indulge in your own victory dance.

- Hug someone.

- Forgive someone.

- Share your news.

- Cross things off.

- Reward yourself.

Your attitude is your altitude.
It is how high you want to fly and how
good you want your day to be.

Practice Gratitude

When was the last time your heart overflowed with gratitude for everything you have? It might have been when you got your dream job, when your child got an award at school, or when you achieved a lifelong goal. As we adapt to the good things in our lives, we can become blind to all we have to be thankful for: a warm bed on a cold night, a delicious meal with people we love, or clean air from the abundance of nature around us.

One of the simplest and most effective ways to ensure we don't take these things for granted is to practice gratitude, to extract the maximum joy and satisfaction from life. Gratitude helps prevent our expectations from becoming an unrealistic burden and keeps our tendency to compare ourselves with others in check. Practice it by counting your blessings each night, keeping a gratitude journal, or writing a gratitude note each day and keeping them in a jar.

Things You Might Be Grateful For

- The hard things in life that have taught you lessons

- Those who are serving you, such as your local barista

- Technology—all the information it gives you and the ways in which it makes your life easier

- Transport—everything that gets you from A to B

- The food you eat

- Your body, your mind, and your soul

- A good night's rest

If we train ourselves to become more aware of the ordinary,
life can very quickly become extraordinary.

Elevate Your Attitude

They say your attitude is your altitude. It determines how high you want to fly and how good you want your day to be. A poor attitude is like a flat tire: if you don't change it, you won't go anywhere. Attitudes are developed by the experiences you encounter in your life. Once you understand them, you can choose your attitude toward your life and your day. Are you choosing self-motivation and self-encouragement, or self-pity and hardship?

How Is Your Attitude Looking?

- Are your words and thoughts positive or negative?

- Do you tend to say, "It's too hard," or, "I'll have a go"?

- Are you open to financial prosperity?

- Are you acknowledging abundance?

- Is your intention of the day—your affirmation—charged with energy and faith?

- Are you saying, "I am so busy, tired, and stressed," or, "I am great"?

- What can you do right now to put yourself in motion, rather than stay stagnant?

- What attitude does your role model have? How can you move toward this right now?

- Do you believe you can change and that a change in attitude could have the greatest impact?

- What is your attitude toward time?

One of the most important parts of this process is to be able to monitor your attitude and the effect it is having on your relationships, career, and well-being. Your attitude affects everyone around you.

Be True to Your Purpose

Staying true to your purpose—your North Star—is the best way to keep your life from fading to gray. Every few months I ask myself the following questions and write down the answers to ensure I remain in the driver's seat of life.

Power Questions

1. What risk would I take if I knew I could not fail? Where is fear holding me back?

2. What are the top five things I treasure in life?

3. If I didn't know my age, how old would I say I am?

4. Where is the line where I stop calculating risk and rewards and start just doing it?

5. How aware am I of the positive or negative energy I am broadcasting?

6. At what time in my recent past have I felt most passionate?

7. How am I manifesting opportunity in my life?

8. What am I avoiding?

9. Am I the author of my thoughts?

10. Am I listening to what I am actually saying?

11. What is the one job, cause, or activity that could get me out of bed happily for the rest of my life? Am I doing it now?

12. What am I committed to?

13. What is my mindfulness practice doing for me?

14. Have I been the kind of friend I'd want to have?

15. What permission do I need or want to move forward?

16. We're always making choices. Am I choosing my story, or is someone else?

Recap

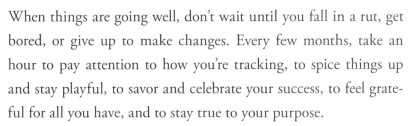

When things are going well, don't wait until you fall in a rut, get bored, or give up to make changes. Every few months, take an hour to pay attention to how you're tracking, to spice things up and stay playful, to savor and celebrate your success, to feel grateful for all you have, and to stay true to your purpose.

Allowing yourself to shine each and every day, as well as honoring yourself for doing so, is a principle worth taking on board. The finishing touches are the finest, smallest details that make the dedication and commitment all worth it. They honor your risks, courage, visions, and attitudes and let the changes you've created move naturally with the tides of life.

Many people report regrets at the end of their life, such as "I wish I had let myself be happier," "I wish I hadn't worked so hard and so much," and "I wish I'd had the courage to live true to myself and not the life others expected of me." Don't let this be you. Taking control and getting into the driver's seat with these easy, small snippets of focus ensures you are always being true to yourself and honoring who you are because you chose to do the work.

Top Tips

- Book a date in your diary every few months to check how you're tracking in life.

- Buy a journal you love to write in and every morning, ask: What's the purpose of today?

- Use all five senses, and be mindful of each sense.

- Be aware of, and appreciate, the ordinary.

- Sing more, hug more, live more.

- Celebrate your successes.

- Start a gratitude jar.

- Spice up your habits.

- Choose an attitude of altitude each day.

- Play, play, play!

- Stay true to your purpose.

- Allow yourself to shine each day.

It's often said that life is a juggling act: family, health, friendships, career . . . The thing to remember is that the career ball is the one that bounces best when it's dropped.

CONCLUSION

Firstly in life, the brain needs a map, a vision, a dream, and goals to focus on that give it purpose each and every day. I am so glad you have answered the questions and have this guide to always refer to for the rest of your life. Once you are on your journey, remember, sometimes life doesn't go the way we plan. Change can turn our plans and our lives upside down and inside out. Sometimes the change can be at a slow pace, and sometimes it will be a total curveball; it will blindside you, completely unexpected, knock you over, and take the wind from beneath your wings.

You then need to accept, adapt, heal, reset yourself, and allow yourself to once again be on your pathway to health, happiness, and success.

Whether the change is in the form of a new child, a new job, a blossoming relationship, a health scare, the loss of a loved one, an accident, or an economic downturn, our ability to learn, heal, repair, pivot, adapt, let go, and change will be the key to our happiness, fulfillment, and success moving forward. Extending your level of flexibility and capacity needs a time-tested, simple, and structured approach when you need to take charge, regain control, and reset your future.

I have been a coach and strategist for twenty years, working with people as they navigate their professional and personal paths, creating incredible twenty-year plans, setting great goals, and improving skills in well-being and self-care rituals that allow them to not burn out. Inevitably, we all also need to deal with change— at work, in intimate relationships, in family dynamics. It can be complicated. I have the pleasure and privilege of working with people as their lighthouse as they navigate the great storms they find themselves in and allowing them to find the calm waters once again. Coming back to our life plan is always the way through.

I know that the ability to adapt, either slowly or quickly by sheer force, to either an opportunity or a crisis, is the key to happiness and inner harmony and to finding our "new normal."

Life is in constant transition. The world changes every day, every hour, every minute. Change is inevitable. It can be positive and exhilarating and take us to a whole new level, full of excitement, awe, and overwhelming joy, and sometimes it can be devastating, painful, and sad and throw us into the depths of loneliness.

During the COVID-19 pandemic, I have worked extensively with those who have gone through the fear, the grief, the loss, the anxiety, the overwhelm, the anger of finding themselves in lockdown. The ability to pivot, to be able to adapt and respond, has been unbelievable. This time, there has been no choice, with everyone thrown in the deep end of a global pandemic. How we chose to respond, on a weekly basis, to our individual circumstances has put all of us to the test. Pure survival, acceptance, nurture, and changing strategically have been of ultimate importance. For some, the growth, opportunities, and unexpected positive changes (like slowing down) could never have been predicted. My family and I took our time and created fresh new plans and also gained great perspective that this too shall pass and we will be returning to our plans, even if they look slightly different.

We all want to be happy. We all want to strive for more. We all want to maximize the personal, professional, and financial potential that life has to offer, but we'd prefer to do so without the stress, exhaustion, and anxiety that is often bundled up with success.

Many of us are overachievers, so we're usually overstimulated, with epic to-do lists, over-connectedness, competing priorities, and crowded social calendars and social media pages.

As much as we want to flourish and succeed, sometimes we will fall off that path. That's okay. This book will bring you back to the basics and remind you of your own personal dream, vision, and goals. It's as simple as that. Always come back and check in with your foundations.

That is the purpose of this book. By understanding the strategies outlined in these pages, you can develop your own personal strategy for living your optimal life. The reality is it is a learning process and new lessons will always unfold, but your foundations are set, and with that, you can live with deep confidence and belief in yourself.

By developing your personal strategy for success, you take action toward living your best life by declaring that it's not enough to simply get by or survive the chaos. That instead, you want to live a remarkable life filled with joy, balance, wholeheartedness, clarity, freedom, gratitude, good health, security, connectedness, purpose, intention, vulnerability, compassion, authenticity, courage, mindfulness, and calm, leaving you free to truly engage in your daily life and enjoy what really matters.

The second purpose of this book is to remind you not to be a passenger in life! And that answering questions, doing the work, and making the plans is what fills our confidence tank. Jump into the driver's seat and live each day with intention, clarity, and purpose, so you can truly engage and enjoy every success.

May you shine bright, no matter where you are in life, and know that you are not alone. Be strong and be gentle. Live calmly and confidently. You've got this.

> With intentional enthusiasm, energy,
> calm confidence, and gratitude,
> Shannah

ACKNOWLEDGMENTS

I'd like to thank all the people who have helped me get to this place:

Thank you to my husband, Michael, who is my rock and my soul mate and is such a support of my twenty years of work in the coaching industry. You have supported my coaching and traveling to speak at conferences, understood when I have gone away to write, and listened to all of my creative ideas for the future and our twenty-year life plan.

Thank you to my children, Jack and Mia Kennedy. You are the greatest gifts I have ever received. You are both strong individuals who are happy, calm, balanced, and respectful. What more could I ask for?

To my clients, who make my life and world so rewarding with the effort you put in. I am truly blown away by the commitment you make to your lives, that you allow me to be your lighthouse, and include me in a part of

your life's journey. You share your innermost thoughts, challenges, and wins with me, and that is something I never take for granted.

To the participants in my self-mastery courses and my corporate lunch-and-learn courses, thank you for being open and willing to take these tools and implement them into your lives.

And to Sylvia Hayse for introducing me to the Beyond Words team. It was so great to meet you virtually in lockdown during the worst of the COVID-19 pandemic and form such a beautiful and trusting relationship. To Michele, Richard, and the rest of Beyond Words, thank you for believing in me. The world awaits us, and I look forward to a long and rewarding relationship together.